Fractional Leadership

Fractional Leadership

LANDING
EXECUTIVE TALENT
YOU THOUGHT
WAS OUT OF REACH

Ben Wolf

HOUNDSTOOTH
PRESS

Fractional Leadership:
Landing Executive Talent You Thought Was Out of Reach

Hardcover ISBN: 978-1-5445-2361-3
Paperback ISBN: 978-1-5445-2359-0
Ebook ISBN: 978-1-5445-2360-6
Audiobook ISBN: 978-1-5445-2358-3

Contents

Introduction

What the Heck Is Fractional Leadership?

WHAT IS THIS BOOK ABOUT AND WHAT DOES "FRACTIONAL" even mean?

You built your company from the ground up, perhaps with a small leadership team at the beginning. You started your business because you thought you could do what you're great at better than other people, or maybe you were just sick of working for someone else and building a business for them. Since you entered the insane world of owning your own business, you sweated, toiled, pivoted 1,000 times, worked to the bone, and now you're thankfully past that grueling startup phase.

It's supposed to get easier now, right? Wrong.

You realized that when you got to ten, twenty, or fifty or more employees, you were in uncharted territory. You knew how to do whatever it is you're great at, whether that's developing apps, graphic design, HVAC installation, or financial services. But you didn't know how to run a small or midsize business. You found out that's a *completely* different skillset.

You started to feel you needed the help of someone who's done this before. Whether your main issues were marketing, sales, operations, finance, or technology, you wanted someone with experience to take over the parts of the business you don't like doing and aren't great at.

It would be great to hire someone with ten or fifteen years' experience to join your leadership team, but at this stage you just don't have the $300,000 for salary, benefits, taxes, and insurance to spend on someone like that. Plus, you don't need that kind of person full-time anyway.

Enter Fractional Leadership˚. Fractional Leadership is simply a slightly fancy way of referring to bringing in an experienced, been-there-done-that executive. That means someone who's already done exactly what you want your business to do—usually multiple times. But they do it without the cost, commitment, or ramp-up time involved in a full-time hire.

There are thousands of Fractional Leaders in the United States alone. They are former full-time CMOs, Chief Sales Officers, COOs, Integrators for companies running on EOS®, CFOs, CTOs, and CIOs who now work part-time for multiple businesses at once.

"Fractional" means that the executive is only with you a portion of the time. They spend a "fraction" of their time with you so that you can get the benefit of their leadership for a fraction of the tremendous cost of a full-time experienced executive.

This book is the first comprehensive guide to Fractional Leadership. It explains who retains Fractional Leaders, the problems they solve, how the engagements work, how to find the right one for you, how to set up an engagement for success, and how the five major categories of Fractional Leadership work.

I've distilled my own experience and everything I've learned about Fractional Leadership into this book so you can learn what Fractional Leadership is, whether it's what you need to break through the ceilings you've been slamming your head against in your business, and how to the get the maximum benefit for your business if you do decide to engage with a Fractional Leader®.

Whom Is This Book For?

You're in the right place if you're the founder, owner, or an executive on the leadership team of a small or midsize business. You have 5–250 people in your company, and you're extremely frustrated because you're hitting the ceiling with the business generally or perhaps in some specific part of it.

Your main blockage may be in your marketing .You've stopped getting the results you used to .You've used up most of your low-hanging-fruit prospects and now you're paying more for worse results.

Perhaps you're frustrated with sales. You're half-managing the sales team yourself and either they or the rest of your company are suffering from neglect. Maybe you hired an underperforming sales manager instead of someone with robust experience to save money, or you elevated your top salesperson to become head of sales. Now you have a bad sales manager and you've lost your top salesperson—the worst of both worlds.

If your challenges are more all-pervasive, it could be an operations issue. You may have underperforming team members, but you don't know what to do about them because you love them as people. You might have too much turnover or your operations can't keep pace with sales. Customers or clients get upset and you have no clear, efficient processes for people to follow to get consistent results. You may lack good data and find yourself always making decisions based on gut instinct and intuition rather than objective facts.

Perhaps your challenge is with finance. Your company grew up with the same person doing your bookkeeping, payroll, A/R, and A/P. But they don't have any previous CFO experience and are now managing your multimillion-dollar revenue. They're great, but they're out of their depth. Or perhaps you're going through a cash crisis or financial transaction like a merger, acquisition, or audit, and you know you need deeper experience and financial leadership.

Your biggest pain point might be technology. The main product you sell to your customers is a proprietary system you developed. But you're relying on a patchwork of freelance developers, an MSP, a VoIP provider, and consultants to keep the operation afloat. But you can't keep your product up to speed on your own anymore. You're one outage or bug away from disaster. Perhaps you use out-of-the-box products but rely on them so thoroughly in the services you provide your clients that you know you need more internal, ongoing expertise to own that part of the business and take it off your hands so you can sleep at night.

Regardless of which part of your business needs the most help, you know you need experienced executive leadership. But you either can't afford it full-time or you aren't ready to hire some of that caliber because of the heavy commitment and long ramp-up time.

Those considering Fractional Leadership typically feel consultants aren't the answer either. Neither you nor anyone on your team has the bandwidth to oversee and fully implement long-term their recommendations. So you don't want to spend the time or significant money involved in retaining a consultant (or *another* consultant).

This book will explain what Fractional Leaders do for you, how they typically structure their engagements, whether Fractional Leadership is the right fit for you, and how to find the right Fractional Leader for your unique business.

Who Am I and Why Am I Writing about Fractional Leadership?

As a Fractional Leader, I know how I've helped clients overcome challenges and blockages they'd suffered from for years and almost come to accept, thinking that they were inevitable. I have also searched for and retained multiple Fractional Leaders on behalf of clients. I've met and interviewed countless other Fractional Leaders through the podcast I host, *Win Win—An Entrepreneurial Community*,[1] and I've learned from and spoken to many others through a lot of networking and connection-building in the entrepreneurial world.

Finally, I learn more and more all the time about Fractional Leadership from both business owners and Fractional Leaders through the "matchmaking" service I provide through www. FractionalLeadership.io. Through this platform, business owners fill out a short profile, and within three days, they receive up to three vetted Fractional Leaders who fit what they're looking for and have availability.

I realized the only information available about Fractional Leadership was on a patchwork of hundreds, if not thousands, of individual Fractional Leader websites spread throughout

---

1 www.FractionalLeadership.io/Podcast

the internet. I saw how manual, ad hoc, and time-consuming it was to search for information about Fractional Leadership. There were no comprehensive books for business owners and leaders explaining what Fractional Leadership is, how it works, whom it's good for, whom it's not good for, and how to find the right Fractional Leader while avoiding the pitfalls and mistakes that cause some engagements to end in failure.

So I decided to write this book to serve as the first book of its type in the history of planet Earth (to my knowledge).

What You're Going to Learn

I found the most useful way to give you the background you need to understand Fractional Leadership, the tools to know whether it's for you, and how to find the best Fractional Leader (FL) for your business was to divide the book into three sections.

Part I (Chapters 1–5) explains what Fractional Leadership is, how it works, how to determine whether it's for you, what kind of FL you need, and how to find the right person.

To give you the context necessary to understand where using an FL might fit into your business, in Chapter 1 I tell the story of what I saw in the business I built without someone who'd done this before on our team. I explain the growth trajectory of Fractional Leadership and how and why it's become so much more popular now, especially after COVID and the associated lockdowns. Finally, I paint a picture of the kind of changes business owners and leadership teams see when using an FL.

Next, in Chapter 2, I explain, at a high level, the theory and experience behind why Fractional Leadership works and what kind of help they give their clients. Hint: the main benefit is usually not simply being a highly skilled worker or an extra set of hands. It's more about leadership and *driving* execution. It means bringing in someone who's already done exactly what you need who can take responsibility for driving execution on fulfilling your greatest need so you don't have to.

What exactly do FLs do and how do their engagements work? I explain the answer to this question in Chapter 3 so you can get a clear, concrete picture of what Fractional Leadership is. This will help you determine whether Fractional Leadership is something you should explore for your own business.

Fractional Leadership is not the right solution for everyone. Even if you're facing the kind of frustrations and challenges an FL solves, your personality, the nature of your company, or your budget may mean you're not an ideal candidate. Chapter 4 teaches you five questions to help you determine whether Fractional Leadership is right for you. If it's not, I offer several alternatives you should consider to help you address the underlying reason you investigated Fractional Leadership to begin with.

Finding the right FL can be a daunting prospect. You must clearly answer several questions before searching for someone so that you can find the kind of person you need. Chapter 5 explains how to determine what kind of FL you need, where to find prospective candidates, and what to ask them so you have the information you need to make the right decision.

In Part II (Chapters 6–11), I explain at a high level how each of the five major types of Fractional Leadership work. In each chapter in this section, I explain what things look like in your business before retaining an FL of each category, what their engagements look like, and some questions to consider asking prospective candidates before making a decision.

I cover Fractional Chief Marketing Officers (FCMOs) in Chapter 6, Chief Sales Officers (FCSOs) in Chapter 7, Chief Operating Officers (FCOOs) in Chapter 8, Fractional Integrators (FIs) in Chapter 9, Chief Financial Officers (FCFOs) in Chapter 10, and Chief Technology Officers (FCTOs) and Chief Information Officers (FCIOs) in Chapter 11.

I bring it all together in Part III where I exhibit my crystal-ball-reading skills in Chapter 12 with a prediction of the future of Fractional Leadership.

Finally, in Chapter 13, I consolidate all the questions and resources mentioned throughout this book into one chapter. This includes several brief checklists and questionnaires you can use to determine whether you're a good candidate for Fractional Leadership, what kind of FL you need, how to find the right FL for you, resources for where to find the right FL for you, how to set up the engagement with your chosen FL for success, and a sample Fractional Leadership agreement.

Now that you know what's in store for you, let's get to it.

Part I

What Fractional Leadership Does for Your Business and How It Works

1.

The Frustration of Hitting the Ceiling When You Haven't Built a Business This Size Before

I WAS BUILDING MY FIRST ENTREPRENEURIAL COMPANY, a mission-driven, tech-powered healthcare startup. I joined the founder as his first full-time hire. He had previously helped run a much larger company, had huge ideas, and was looking for a place to build everything he dreamed of. I built most of our company's operations, and we thankfully grew to the largest healthcare agency of our type in the entire state of New York in under three years.

Although that sounds great, not everything was unicorns and rainbows. As we grew much bigger, attrition among our clients became a major issue. Patients chose caregivers, and then when those caregivers couldn't work for them anymore for some reason, the patients sought other solutions, such as traditional home care, and dropped off the program.

We hit other problems too. We depended on a constant supply of new leads and did significant marketing. But despite the amounts we were spending, a disturbingly large portion of those leads couldn't be attributed to any particular marketing campaign. Furthermore, we strongly suspected that people attributed to one campaign or source really got there in response to another. For instance, let's say someone heard about us on the radio, then saw our subway ad, and later that week saw us on the side of a bus, and then finally, they Googled us. Boom, it's a lead attributable to Google pay-per-click! We were therefore forced to make critical marketing decisions with a lot at stake based on gut instinct rather than data.

Internally, we had people issues. Although we cared a lot, the members of the leadership team were insanely busy and underwater with everything we were accomplishing. We didn't have enough time to train new people. They were thrown in to learn from others who were also very busy. People got upset, and we didn't know what to do. The problem was that even though we on the leadership team were very smart (just being honest), cared a lot, and had a lot of talent, none of us had ever *run* a business with a hundred employees before! We felt frustrated.

We tried hiring a consultant to tell us how to solve our problems. We paid him a lot of money and invested a lot of time with him. He came into our office and interviewed dozens of employees, mapped out what our current processes were, and invested tremendous effort in understanding where our bottlenecks were. In the end, he gave us a sixty-page tome outlining all the changes he recommended and why.

Despite the herculean effort he put in and through no fault of his own, we ignored the vast majority of his recommendations. Why? Because we felt he simply did not understand the nature of our business, our clientele, our values, and what was important to us. Plus, we were already underwater and could not devote the bandwidth necessary to implement the changes he recommended even if we wanted to.

We tried the same thing with a marketing consultant. He never really *got* what we and our clients were all about. So we returned to doing marketing all on our own again. We saw much better results than he was able to provide.

That's why I call what consultants do "drive-by consulting." They drive past, throw a list of recommendations at you, and then drive right on by. Most consultants cannot stay with you to get to know the company, its business, people, and values. Nor can they stay with you to drive execution of the solutions they recommend (though some do offer to lead implementation for a hefty sum). The nature of the engagement, or cost, usually make it unworkable.

So what could we do?

I did not learn the answer to this question until I became an FL myself.

After I left that first entrepreneurial company, I knew I loved building businesses and wanted to do it on a much larger scale, full-time. In the management framework we used at the startup, Entrepreneurial Operating System® (EOS®), we call someone who functions as a general manager, COO, or president an Integrator. That was the kind of work that got my juices flowing.

I heard about the concept of an FI from reading *Rocket Fuel: The One Essential Combination That Will Get You More of What You Want from Your Business* by Gino Wickman and Mark C. Winters, which is all about the Visionary-Integrator relationship. A light bulb went off. An FI is like an outsourced COO. That's what I wanted to do! So I hung up my shingle, so to speak, and soon found one client, and then another, and then another.

At the same time, I met many other experienced, C-level executives of all types, who were working for multiple clients just like I was. I now call these types of people Fractional Leaders® (FLs for short). The five most common types I found were Fractional (1) Chief Marketing Officers (FCMOs), (2) Chief Sales Officers (FCSOs), (3) operations leaders like Chief Operating Officers (FCOOs) or Integrators (FIs), (4) Chief Financial Officers (FCFOs), and (5) technology people like Chief Information Officers (FCIOs) and Chief Technology Officers (FCTOs).

I met some of these FLs through my podcast, *Win Win—An Entrepreneurial Community*. I was introduced to others through networking within the EOS world. One relationship led to another, and as I met more and more people, I began to realize how large and growing the world of Fractional Leadership® was.

One of my guests on the *Win Win* podcast, Jim Muehlhausen, founder of the FCSO licensing firm SalesQB, explains it like this: "The scourge of small business is fractionalization. How many receptionists do you need full-time? 1.3. How many assemblers do you need? 4.7. You never need a whole person, right? You need a piece of a whole person. And so we as small business owners have always dealt with that by making people do nine jobs."[2] That's what led him to create SalesQB as a licensed system to help FCSOs run sales fractionally for small and midsize businesses.

I see every day with my own clients what a difference my own Fractional Leadership makes. Before I joined the team,

---

2 "How to Keep Your Business and Get a Better Lifestyle by Half Retiring: Interview with Jim Muehlhausen," *Win Win—An Entrepreneurial Community* podcast, episode 61, September 14, 2020, https://podcasts. apple.com/us/podcast/061-how-to-keep-your-business-get-better-lifestyle/ id1465488607?i=1000491201673.

they were hitting the same ceiling I had hit on my own entrepreneurial journey. I call this ceiling the Entrepreneurial Catch-22. Most entrepreneurs who survive the startup phase experience some variation of the same thing. They can't scale without bringing on an experienced C-level leader, but they also can't afford someone like that until after they've scaled. Working with them as an FL helps them break through the ceiling and escape the Entrepreneurial Catch-22.

What Is Fractional Leadership?

Fractional Leadership means engaging with an experienced C-level executive who's already scaled an organization like yours. You make them a part of your leadership team as an FL to fast-track your ability to break through the ceilings holding you back for a fraction of what it costs to hire someone like that full-time.

Why do so many founder-led businesses hit the ceiling again and again after passing through the startup phase? I believe it is usually because the people on the founding leadership team have never run a business that size before. And they certainly haven't led a business as big as they *want* theirs to become.

The data backs this up. Contrary to the stereotype of entrepreneurs as experienced, savvy serial business starters, about 90 percent of startups are founded by people who never started a business before.[3] If you're feeling alone, like there's something wrong with you because you don't know how to solve

---

3   Only 10 percent of new businesses are founded by serial entrepreneurs. Kathryn L. Shaw and Anders Sørensen, "The Productivity Advantage of Serial Entrepreneurs," NBER Working Paper 23320, April 2017, http://www.nber.org/papers/w23320.

the problems your business is facing now, you're not. You're just like 90 percent of the other small and midsize business owners out there.

My first FI client was a media company that creates ad placements on popular websites. In doing so, the media company gives their clients more revenue than they could get on their own. They grew 25 percent revenue in the first quarter I worked with them. This was not because I have magical or mystical powers, or because I'm an ad tech guru. It was because I'd built a business from smaller than theirs to much bigger before. I knew where the pitfalls were and what challenges they were facing, and I'd already learned what to do through trial and error. I helped them skip past the learning curve. Because they had me on board, there was no need for them to reinvent the wheel. I helped them gain the focus and discipline they needed to immediately attack some of the low-hanging fruit—the little things that were holding them back. They simply didn't know how to do it.

Another of my clients was a cybersecurity firm that contracts with federal agencies. Their sales team had been hitting the ceiling for a while, and no matter what they tried, they couldn't break through. When I suggested they consider an FCSO, the CEO was initially hesitant even though he had already retained me as an FL!

I assured him he would get a lot further by trying it out than he would continuing to bang his head against the wall. So he bit the bullet and interviewed three FCSOs I introduced him to, each with relevant federal contracting experience.

Fast forward three months later. Kristen McGarr of Adroit Insights, the FCSO he chose, had embedded herself with the team on the days she spent there. She cost much less than the salary, bonus, benefits, and taxes they would have paid hiring someone full-time, and as a vendor, she started and ramped up in weeks, not months, like a major executive hire would have. She hit the ground running, learned how things worked, and used her past success and knowledge to restructure the sales process. She knew what was important to track, coached the existing team to dramatically increase their closed sales, and hired and trained new members of the team to position them to grow. They grew more in the first year after retaining her than they had in the previous four.

Outsourcing Customer Service—Fine. But C-level Leadership?

People know about outsourcing and utilizing freelancers for less-skilled activities like answering phones, data entry, and virtual assistance. In fact, the global outsourcing market for IT alone was $333.7 billion in 2019.[4] But it sounds crazy to think of outsourcing C-level executive leadership. Right?

But the truth is that Fractional Leadership isn't as foreign a concept as it initially appears. There are elements of it in the way we have been using attorneys and accountants for decades, if not centuries. We consult with someone about the most sensitive parts of our business and accept their guidance and leadership in our financial, compliance, and legal decision making even though they aren't full-time employees and only bill us by the hour.

---

4 "Global IT Outsourcing Market 2020–2025: Growing Demand to Efficiency and Scalable IT Infrastructure," Business Wire, August 10, 2020, https://www.businesswire.com/news/home/20200810005303/en/ Global-Outsourcing-Market-2020-2025---Growing-Demand.

If your business is hitting the ceiling and you and your leadership team just aren't sure what to do about it but aren't scaled big enough to bring the experience and expertise you need in-house, full-time, you aren't alone. According to the Organisation for Economic Co-operation and Development (OECD), there are over 4 million businesses with 10–249 employees in the United States alone. And let me remind you, the vast majority of those business owners have never done this before either.

How and Why Is Fractional Leadership an Emerging Trend?

Why are more people hiring FLs? Lonnie Martin, CEO coach and Vistage Chair, writes:

> Oftentimes proven CxO experience can result in five to twenty times in company returns. What's the value of a bankruptcy a bookkeeper didn't see coming versus a CFO who spotted the possibility quarters in advance? What's the value of a highly targeted marketing campaign that discovers or creates a competitive advantage that changes a company's win rate from 20 to 50 percent and at higher prices? What's the value of never missing a delivery? What's the value of systems and/or operational efficiencies that give your company cost leadership?[5]

Forbes reported that Kent Huffman, founder of FCFO firm DigiMark Partners, said:

---

5   Lonnie Martin, "Biz Smarts: Outsourcing Executive Talent Can Be a Wise Strategy for Small, Growing Companies," Biz Journals, August 9, 2018, https://www.bizjournals.com/sacramento/news/2018/08/09/biz-smarts-outsourcing-executive-talent-can-be-a.html.

Fractional CMOs are most often the best fit for mid-market organizations that don't need or can't afford a permanent, full-time marketing leader but would benefit from the knowledge and strategic leadership that a short-term, experienced, and accomplished CMO could bring to the company. Beyond serving as a part-time addition to the C-suite, fractional CMOs usually offer other services to their clients, such as… advising the CEO on marketing related issues and opportunities, managing strategic marketing initiatives, conducting strategy workshops, coaching/mentoring lower-level marketing staffers, and conducting marketing audits.[6]

All of this explains why it's beneficial to so many business owners to retain an FL. But I've noticed a profound uptick in interest from potential clients in the past year, and I've heard the same thing from many other FLs I know. What's driving the explosive growth of Fractional Leadership?

We find ourselves at the crest of a large and growing Fractional Leadership market, poised at the convergence of three emerging trends: (1) post-COVID financial pressure, (2) more experienced C-level leaders "going fractional," and (3) the world has crossed the "event horizon" beyond which collaboration technology has irrevocably made virtual work more effective and desirable for many.

Let's examine each of these three trends.

---

6 Kimberly A. Whitler, "The Outsourced Executive: A Growing Leadership Staffing Solution," Forbes, July 28, 2015, https://www.forbes.com/sites/kimberlywhitler/2015/07/28/the-outsourced-c-level-executive-a-growing-leadership-trend/#4f53cc9c5da1.

More Results for Less Money When Things Are Tough

First, these are tough times for almost everyone. People are contending with months and possibly years or longer of pandemic, lockdowns, social distancing, and safety restrictions. Some fortunate businesses grew and thrived, whether they pivoted or were fortuitously well-positioned. But most I spoke with saw revenue drop anywhere from 10–90 percent in the first few months of 2020. Small business revenues dropped an average of 52 percent.[7] This only accelerated the demand for Fractional Leadership to solve small businesses' "diseconomies of scale"— that is, decreased efficiency as they grew. More about that later.

"Contingent labor increased with the economic downturn this year, including fractional leadership—where executives lend part of their time to a company. Fractional executives are beneficial for both sides—the company gets the expertise of execs with less cost and helps prevent burnout for the executive grinding through the same problems daily," said Ray Culver, the SVP: Head of Growth of TalentNow.[8]

People became very sensitive to the fact that they cannot take their revenue for granted because circumstances and rules change constantly. Few have an appetite to take on expensive new hires unless it is absolutely necessary. Teresa Renaud, an FCSO affiliated with SalesQB, explains it this way: "A very common problem affecting all small businesses

---

7   Samson Haileyesus, "Small Business Revenue Dropped 52 Percent during Pandemic, Biz2Credit Data Reveals," Small Business Trends, August 8, 2020, https://smallbiztrends.com/2020/08/biz2credit-small-business-financial-health-survey-july-2020.html.

8   Kristina Knight, "How to Continue—and Improve—Remote Work Options," BizReport, December 29, 2020, http://www.bizreport.com/2020/12/how-to-continue---and-improve---remote-work-options.html.

is this concept of a diseconomy of scale. It's hard to afford expert resources when you have smaller teams or a smaller organization. Fractional service providers actually plug in to that problem. That problem is their competitive thorn and the Fractional Leader is their competitive weapon."[9]

Yet people cannot grow the way they want to or at the desired speed without experienced leadership.

I believe this is why more and more people are reaching out to me and other FLs I know. They can onboard experienced executive leadership far faster, with less commitment, and while paying much less than they would in salary, benefits, and taxes for a full-time hire of that caliber.

More Experienced Executives "Going Fractional"

The second factor driving the expanding adoption of Fractional Leadership is that more executives are "going fractional." Why?

A UK study in 2017 surprisingly found that the largest category of gig economy work (26 percent) was at the *highest* skill level, rather than the lowest as we might have expected.[10] According to *Harvard Business Review*, leaders increasingly go independent because it allows them to do more satisfying work with a broader range of clients for higher compensation and

---

9 "How to Free Up from Half-Managing an Underperforming Sales Team: Interview with Teresa Renaud," *Win Win—An Entrepreneurial Community* podcast, episode 54, July 21, 2020, https://podcasts.apple.com/us/podcast/054-how-to-free-up-from-half-managing-underperforming/id1465488607?i=1000485649903.

10 Brhmie Balaram, Josie Warden, and Fabian Wallace-Stephens, "Good Gigs: A Fairer Future for the UK's Gig Economy," RSA Reports, April 26, 2017, https://medium.com/rsa-reports/good-gigs-a-fairer-future-for-the-uks-gig-economy-f2485a22de09.

with more flexibility.[11] Jim Muehlhausen, author of *Half-Retire* and founder of SalesQB (a licensed system for independent FCSOs), shared with me that many leaders go out on their own because they know that pressures on businesses to cut costs paint a target on the highest paid employees' heads. In fact, based on data collected in September 2020, Upwork reported that 75 percent of people who left full-time positions to work freelance made the same or more money than they did when they were employed.[12]

Kevin McMahon, of Colorado-based Vertex CFO, decided to help multiple clients as an FCFO after becoming frustrated with the lack of long-term stability over the course of four different full-time CFO roles.

Kevin started to see a pattern in his full-time CFO roles. He improved or turned around an organization and shepherded them through remarkable growth. Then the owners would sell the company or merge with another entity which would inevitably replace the financial leadership with their own CFO. For example, in one of his previous roles, Kevin served as VP of Finance at a technology company for over four years. During that time, he worked with the organization's leadership team to grow the company's revenue from $70 to $120 million and helped effectuate its international expansion to diversify risk in case the American market softened. When the company sold to a private equity buyer, new ownership saw Kevin as the vanguard of the old order and ultimately let him go.

---

11 Dena McCallum, Susa J. Ashford, and Briana Barker Caza, "Why Consultants Quit Their Jobs to Go Independent," *Harvard Business Review*, July 15, 2019, https://hbr.org/2019/07/why-consultants-quit-their-jobs-to-go-independent.

12 https://www.upwork.com/documents/freelance-forward-2020.

Kevin shares that full-time finance leadership is "not an ideal scenario if you want to incentivize people to want to get to the top of leadership when it comes to finance." He also loves the greater variety he gets as an FL. "It'd be great if I could get involved in raising money again. Or do a startup again. In a [full-time] corporate role, there's no such thing. It's very much a running and repeating type of business."

Personally, I find that at a certain point in my career, I got bored building and running only one company all the time. I don't think one can become a successful FL without first building one or more companies full-time, in-house. But at this point, that's not what gives me the satisfaction I'm looking for. I've heard the same thing from others as well.

Many people who enjoy and are good at marketing, sales, finance, operations, or technology usually want to focus on that, and don't want the risk of having to find clients, especially if they have families to support. That is normal, completely understandable, and represents the majority of C-level executives.

But an increasing number of leaders, especially in the entrepreneurial space, are taking the leap to go out on their own.

We've Crossed the Remote Work Event Horizon

Before COVID, I worked on business development, trying to find FI clients regardless of whether they lived in my local area (New York City and the surrounding area) or anywhere else in the world.

The problem I faced was that people couldn't imagine working at the leadership level with someone they couldn't sit with eyeball-to-eyeball. Many just could not get their heads around the idea of a remote FL even if they understood and believed that Fractional Leadership would have propelled their businesses far further than they could have on their own.

Everything changed in March 2020. People were literally forced to have all their employees work remotely, including leadership. As Zoom's chief product officer Odel Gal said about the lockdown, "All the people that were resistant to using the technology were forced to use it."[13] Most discovered that the sky did not fall down and productivity did not plummet when people worked from home.

After a few months of remote work ,I saw a dramatic shift in attitude .When people got their bearings ,they realized they were not limited by geography when putting together their best team .Starting around May ,2020 I and many other FLs I know began getting far more inquiries and filled up our client rosters much more quickly than we had before.

Increased cultural acceptance of remote work combined with the increasing effectiveness of collaboration tools like Zoom ,Monday.com ,Slack ,Asana ,and the like has changed the work landscape .I refer to these phenomena as crossing the" remote work event horizon".

The term *event horizon* refers to the demarcation line around a black hole beyond which an object can pass by without being sucked in. But if something crosses within a black hole's event horizon, even light, there's no turning back. When leaders were forced to acclimate to people working remotely, they even realized that without time around the water cooler, so to speak, their people were about 13 percent

---

13 Adam Clark Estes, "What Comes after Zoom Fatigue," Vox Recode, July 17, 2020, https://www.vox.com/recode/21314793/ zoom-fatigue-video-chat-facebook-google-meet-microsoft-teams.

more productive than they were in the office.[14] Even my own former company, which resisted my efforts to perform remote work experiments, decided not to return to in-person work even after it became permitted safety-wise. *Forbes* now claims that its own prediction that over 50 percent of the workforce would be remote by 2027 was too conservative.[15]

Because remote work is now so prevalent, even at the executive level, bringing in experienced Fractional Leadership to solve the Entrepreneurial Catch-22 is much easier for business owners to wrap their heads around. Mark Thacker, president of Sales Xceleration, writes that "before the pandemic, it would have been difficult to imagine that some companies would completely shift from in-office setups to remote work in a matter of months…Many of my company's clients assumed they couldn't manage their sales teams remotely and that they couldn't sell virtually in an effective manner. As is the case with most assumptions, they weren't validated; they were the 'head trash' that comes with guessing what is and isn't possible before actually testing beliefs."[16]

I think we have crossed the remote work event horizon. Once everyone was forced to try out remote work for several months, it let the genie out of the bottle. There will always be some people who are hardwired to hate not working in person. And that's fine. Very often, people can find an FL in

---

14 Nicholas Bloom, James Liang, John Roberts, and Zhichun Jenny Ying, "Does Working from Home Work? Evidence from a Chinese Experiment," The Quarterly Journal of Economics 130, no. 1 (February 2015), https://www.gsb.stanford.edu/faculty-research/publications/does-working-home-work-evidence-chinese-experiment.

15 See https://www.forbes.com/sites/forbesbusinesscouncil/2020/09/22/five-reasons-why-the-remote-workforce-wont-return-to-the-office/?sh=3274943c594a.

16 See https://born2invest.com/articles/remote-work-revolution-squash-stigma-part-time-leaders/.

their own city. If, before the pandemic, 15 percent of business owners would have considered a remote, C-level FL, I estimate that perhaps 30–50 percent are now open to it.

Next

We have now introduced the Fractional Leadership concept and seen, at a high level, how bringing an experienced executive onto your leadership team fractionally can get you most of the results you would by hiring someone full-time but with a much faster ramp-up time, less long-term commitment, and for much less cost.

That sounds interesting. But how does Fractional Leadership really work? What does it look like? How do you know whether it's for you? Read the next chapter to find out.

2.

How Experienced Fractional Leaders Break Through Your Biggest Challenges So You Can Enjoy What You've Built

WHAT DOES IT MEAN FOR YOUR BUSINESS TO HAVE AN experienced leader swoop in when you're stuck and guide you to your destination ?A strong leader who has" been there and done that "knows what to do and how to inspire your troops to charge into the breach together with them.

Nothing illustrates this more clearly than the story of Brigadier General Norman "Dutch" Cota.

Everything went wrong with the Allies' D-Day invasion on June 6, 1944. Almost all of the tanks sent to support the invasion were destroyed or sunk before reaching land. The Allied bombers missed the German fortifications. The Germans shot most of the Allied troops in their boats or on the beach, and many others drowned before getting to shore.

The few soldiers who survived the passage across the deadly beach at Omaha gathered below the seawall. A US Army after-action report called even the few soldiers who made it to the seawall, "inert, leaderless and almost incapable of action." They had no idea how to scale the bluffs and cross the barbed wire so they could attack the German positions and thereby enable the Allied forces to cross the beach and begin their invasion.

Fifty-one-year-old Cota finally reached the seawall and knew the invasion would fail if no one led the way. While everyone else huddled beneath the bluffs, Cota began walking in search of a good breaching position. Seeing him take action, other soldiers joined in. While some were hit, the general assigned one man to cover him while another man used a torpedo to blow through the double-apron barbed wire blocking access to the bluff.

After the first man to go through the gap in the wire was shot, everyone else froze up. Cota knew what he had to do. He charged through the gap and survived, thereby inspiring other troops by his own example. He gathered the soldiers who made it to the other side and led the first successful infantry assault on the German positions in the Allies' Normandy campaign.

Although nothing we do in business compares even remotely to the Allied assault on D-Day, Cota's story illustrates how experienced leadership turns the tide in a dedicated team's efforts to achieve a goal despite any obstacle. Through your business, you've brought something into the world that no one else could. But now, you're stuck under a seawall, not sure how to move forward. An FL can be your General Cota to lead your troops to break through the ceiling you're hitting and conquer the next stage of your growth.

Why It Works

Natalie Franke, co-founder of The Rising Tide Society and author of the just-released book *Built to Belong*, leads a community of over 70,000 business owners in creative industries like floral design, graphic arts, and filmmaking. I spoke with her to find out what kind of patterns or trends she's seen in the large swathe of the business world she works with. Natalie says:

> What I've seen happen is scaling growth. When you ask the winners in these industry arenas, whoever has become the top dog in their particular niche, like floral design, they have outsourced specific segments of their business. Those who scaled from the $250,000 level to $3 million or more, have brought in an experienced expert onto their team, very often in the area of financial leadership, strategy, cash flow for seasonal business, and accounting.

The biggest reason Fractional Leadership works is you're bringing someone on your side who's already gotten past the point where you're stuck—and they've usually done so multiple times. They shortcut you around bottlenecks and obstacles so you can break through and go way beyond where you could on your own.

Wil Schroter, founder and CEO of Startups.com, the world's largest startup launch platform and cohost of the *Startup Therapy Podcast*, explains that in the startup world, Fractional Leadership "is just called hiring."

> There's no way I could possibly afford the kind of COO or CMO I need. I bring them on in exchange for maybe a quarter point of equity because early equity is the only kind of currency I have at that point. And the truth is that I don't need that CMO to run my pay-per-click anyway. I can find someone on fiverr to

do the grunt work. What I need is for her to tell me what's around every corner, which company I need a partnership with, and "By the way, here are the contacts you need to talk to." She'll send an email that will take fifteen minutes of her time and save me a year of my time. That guidance and those relationships are worth their weight in gold.

For people who are used to having to figure everything out for themselves, it can almost feel like cheating. They worry they're doing something wrong by bypassing the obstacles and skipping straight to effective (though often not easy) solutions. Although this feeling is natural, it causes them unnecessary pain and makes their progress toward their own dreams much longer and harder than it has to be.

Kwame Christian, Esq., Director of the American Negotiation Institute and author of *Finding Confidence in Conflict*, told me that he uses an FCFO in his company because it allows him to bring extensive experience and an objective perspective into his business but without the full-time cost:

My Fractional CFO manages the entire financial side of our business. He has that high-level expertise, but we don't need to pay for full-time.

His benefit is also objectivity. I think it's easier to be more objective about the company when you have a little bit of separation. My background is in psychology, and I do some implicit bias training from time-to-time because bias is just a natural state of the human mind. I have preconceived notions about my own business. So I tell him, "Listen, I'm biased. This is the way I'm seeing it, but I'm probably missing something. What am I missing?" He can see things a lot more objectively. It's been really helpful to have that outside influence.

I spoke about what Fractional Leadership means for entrepreneurs with Christal Jackson, founder of Mosaic Genius, which builds sustainable wealth ecosystems in communities of color by connecting and curating gatherings for underserved entrepreneurs and venture capitalists. She used the Fractional Leadership model early on in the growth of her company so she could focus on what she was good at. She told me:

> We now have a COO. She was extremely helpful. She was very experienced and was capping off a very full career. She helped us with strategy and to set up systems and processes that I didn't have at the time. This was critical for my overall business management and growth. Having her come in to manage things so I could focus on business development was a huge weight lifted off my shoulders because as an entrepreneur, you tend to get personally involved in how everything gets done. I was able to free up my brain and think more about the type of clients we actually wanted.

Jennifer Zick is the founder and CEO of Authentic Brand, an FCMO firm serving growing businesses throughout the United States and globally. Jennifer explains that the role of an FCMO is not to individually implement all the tactics of marketing (SEO, web development, content, events, creative, etc.) but to integrate all the people, programs, and processes of the marketing function. An FCMO provides strategic guidance as a member of the executive team and as a leader of marketing employees, agency partners, and contract freelancers. An FCMO ensures that all efforts are tied together cohesively and directed toward healthy growth outcomes. An FCMO leads, manages, and ensures accountability—filling a key role in the organization and building a strong marketing engine. Ultimately, an FCMO helps the business move more confidently toward a full-time executive marketing hire/promotion or toward a new chapter of growth through mergers and acquisition.[17]

Jason Prentice, FI and co-founder of Outcomes COO, came into one small business that was hitting the ceiling because they had several people on the team whom everyone liked but who had simply passed their performance limit. The company couldn't grow any more. To make the organization's progress more concrete, he began measuring employees' Net Promoter Score®, or NPS®, every month. NPS is a way of measuring people's positive feelings about a company or brand. When he started, several people in this small business were "detractors" or, at best, "neutral."

The prevailing wisdom on the leadership team was that replacing any of these beloved underperforming employees would destroy the company's already fragile morale because it would take away people whom others liked a lot and

17 "How to Have a Marketing Strategy rather than Random Acts of Marketing: Jennifer Zick Interview," *Win Win—An Entrepreneurial Community* podcast, episode 13, August 19, 2019, Jennifer Zick, https://podcasts.apple.com/us/podcast/013-how-to-have-marketing-strategy-rather-than-random/id1465488607?i=1000447240281.

make them more afraid for their own job security. Because Jason had seen this pattern before, he encouraged them to make a change with some of their low-performing but well-liked employees.

After replacing those positions with new team members, something they did not expect happened. The company's NPS went up rather than down! Within a matter of months, the entire team were promoters or people in the "passive" category and their client satisfaction was also approaching the highest level it had been in years.

Leader, Not Worker Bee

Tactical, frontline-type work is a distraction from FLs' main value proposition. FCSOs, for example, generally do not make their own sales. FCOOs do not personally lead highly technical system rollouts. And FCFOs do not personally do your bookkeeping, A/P, and payroll. Instead, FLs set up systems and processes that cause the people in your organization to do their jobs far more effectively than before. They then train and oversee those teams. This ultimately gets you far more results than one person, even one who is very skilled, can accomplish on their own. The power of FLs is their experience and ability to focus your organization's resources on your priorities.

You probably built your business by being a "doer" who gets as much accomplished as is humanly possible. Your leadership team always did the same. The problem is, as the saying goes, "What got you here isn't going to get you there." Even though the "all hands on deck," "get 'er done" culture got you past the critically dangerous startup phase, you've now reached the stage in your business where that does not work anymore. Isn't that why you're frustrated and reading about Fractional Leadership in the first place?

Get Focused on the Right Things

Jim[18] founded Appleton Wealth Management on the strength of his relationships in the Twin Cities, Minnesota. He built up a staff to help him scale and began managing investments, retirement assets, insurance, and tax planning for many of the high-net-worth people in central Minnesota and beyond. He and his team worked very hard for their clients.

However, eventually Appleton stopped growing. Its inability to scale beyond a certain point frustrated Jim, so he retained Jerry Rick as an FI/COO to spend about a day-and-a-half per week with them. Jerry soon realized that because it did not focus on any one type of asset management, Appleton had no particularly compelling value proposition above and beyond what any other wealth management company could promise. Not only that, because it landed the vast majority of its clients because of Jim's reputation and relationships (and there was only one of him), the whole business wasn't scalable.

Jerry knew from experience that when you try to be all things to all people, there's nothing to set you apart. He helped Appleton narrow down the focus to investment management because they could not excel at that *and* insurance and tax planning. With the new, narrower focus, Jerry helped Jim go national within Appleton's newly defined specialty. They

---

18 Names have been changed.

sponsored conferences, marketed, and dramatically grew their assets under management, requiring them to hire more people to meet the new demand. The team also used its extensive experience in investment management to develop webinars, trainings, content marketing strategies, and tools to help clients and prospects while simultaneously establishing Appleton's own expertise and reputation.

Jim broke through the growth ceiling he'd hit because he brought Jerry on board, even though he didn't need someone full-time at the beginning. Once Jerry finished overseeing the implementation of the initial substantive changes necessary to get Appleton to the next level, he helped Jim find and train a full-time Integrator/COO to replace him.

Whether you use an FCSO to focus your sales process and message on what resonates with your target market, an FCFO to make the right decisions based on financial experience, analysis, and data, or an FCTO to build and iterate the right product, focus is key. Because FLs have seen what works and know how to drive implementation, people use them to focus their limited resources on the right things for maximum impact and scalability.

Next

You now have an idea of what Fractional Leadership is, why it's gaining so much more prominence among business owners, and the basics of why it works to get people past that Entrepreneurial Catch-22. You know you can't scale without experienced executive leadership, but you can't afford or aren't ready to commit that kind of leadership full-time until after you've scaled.

How exactly do FL engagements work? How much time does an FL spend with you? How much does it cost? What exactly will they do for you? For the answers to these questions and more, stay tuned for the next chapter.

3.

What Fractional Leadership Engagements Look Like So You Know Exactly What to Expect

CONSIDER THE FOLLOWING EXAMPLE OF ONE BUSINESS owner's experience to better understand what Fractional Leadership engagements look like.

Jack[19] owns a design construction firm called Built to Design. The firm focuses on medical offices, employs about forty people, and has $14–16 million in annual revenue. His attention to detail and nearly obsessive commitment to quality work led him to essentially teach his sales, design, and construction teams that *all* decisions had to go through him. Every deal required his approval and input. He was intimately involved in design proposals and construction projects. Mistakes were unacceptable and his people did not really know how to predict what he would consider a mistake. It was safer to run everything through him for approval.

Built to Design had hit a blockage. They tried to continue growing, but no matter what they did, they simply could not

---

19 Names have been changed.

push past that $14–$16 million revenue ceiling. But they could not figure out why this was happening.

Last year, Jack took his family on a vacation for the first time in about five years. He and his wife had young children, so they went to Disney World in Orlando and on a Disney cruise. They explored the Disney parks, relaxed, and went swimming at the resort's pool. During the cruise, the entertainment and activities were truly magical. Disney indeed lived up to its reputation. They had an amazing time. It was so refreshing because much of the time, particularly on the cruise, there was little or no cell phone reception, so he was able to truly enjoy the time with his family without interruption.

Well rested and rejuvenated, Jack returned to Built to Design. To his horror, Jack discovered that basically nothing had happened in his absence. Not only had his team made no sales, but they had also lost several of their prospects who needed to move quickly. When the salespeople or designers could not move their projects forward, the potential customers simply went elsewhere.

This was a huge wake-up call for Jack and his team. They finally realized that because he had made himself indispensable to every single sales, design, and operational decision, he was the bottleneck creating the ceiling against which his firm was hitting its collective head. The team hadn't built any processes or metrics to ensure that people made sales, completed designs, and constructed medical offices the right way, every time, with or without Jack's involvement.

Inspired by the wake-up call, Jack retained Kendley Davenport, President of the FCSO firm Outsourced Sales Pros, to act as the company's Head of Sales. Kendley created a true sales process by clearly documenting the right and best way to do things. Kendley helped the sales team establish metrics so they had specific actions they knew to take every day and every week to ensure they made enough sales to achieve their goals. He helped the design team do the same thing.

Because of the systems, processes, and metrics Kendley helped the company put into place and which he oversaw, Jack was able to start redirecting salespeople's and designers' inquiries to the right people. He started taking himself out of the equation so the team could sell design construction contracts without him. They started to see their revenues break through that $16 million ceiling and finally had the bandwidth to expand into other types of construction.

At this point, you understand at a high level why bringing someone onto your leadership team who's built a business like yours before will help you. The next few subsections of this chapter will explain what a Fractional Leadership engagement looks like and how exactly it actually works.

Accountabilities and Deliverables

You and your FL will agree to certain deliverables or areas of accountability and a time frame in which you expect to see the results you want. This is a critical element of any type of Fractional Leadership engagement.

Here are some examples of the deliverables one FCSO included in an agreement:

- Lead sales team to achieve the company's already-established targets for the year

- Participate in weekly leadership team meetings

- Document the sales process and ensure the team is trained in it and follows it

- Determine and implement measurables to which she will hold herself and the members of the sales team accountable

- Collaborate with the head of marketing to ensure all efforts are absolutely in tandem

- Evaluate current CRM/technology and improve or revamp as appropriate

Personally, as an FI, I hold myself accountable to achieving four things for clients:

- Lead weekly leadership meetings. In these meetings, I hold each member of the leadership accountable to their quarterly priorities and to their measurables. During these meetings, I also facilitate maximum effectiveness and efficiency in their issue-solving discipline to ensure they solve issues at the root and for good.

- Hold Same Page Meetings™ with the company's Visionary (an EOS® term that usually refers to the CEO). I use these to ensure that the Visionary and I are 100 percent on the same page. This provides us the opportunity to resolve issues related to other members of the leadership team, as well as any other challenges keeping him or her up at night.

- Miscellaneous execution. Depending on the needs of the company, I may take on a quarterly goal of my own, like filling a leadership team seat or documenting a core process and ensuring members of the relevant department are measured and managed according to that process. Alternatively, I may coach other members of the leadership team to ensure they maximally achieve their quarterly priorities.

- Participate in EOS sessions with their EOS Implementer®. Most of the clients I work with have implemented the EOS management framework with the help of an outside EOS Implementer. I participate in their quarterly and annual leadership team sessions with this Implementer as a fellow member of the leadership team.

You and your FL will structure the accountabilities based on the FL's proven process and your own unique needs. The important thing is that you and your FL get absolutely on the same page regarding the deliverables or accountabilities so there is no misunderstanding or crossed wires later on.

On-site versus Remote

For those considering working with an FL virtually, how can that work if they aren't physically on the carpet with the rest of the team? How can it work if they can't talk to you eye-to-eye to really get a feel for who you are and how you feel?

Many of the assumptions underlying this question are based on a theoretical fear not grounded in what virtual engagements are really like. For many business owners, the COVID-19 lockdowns exploded this concern.

At one of my prior companies, one of the many hats I wore was taking care of everything involved in moving us from one new office to another because of our fast growth. To slow down our constant need to move into new offices, I periodically pushed for moving at least some of our workforce to remote work or at least conducting a serious experiment with it. (All of this happened before COVID.) The rest of the leadership team was incredulous. How can we create accountability for people who aren't physically in the office with us? How can we keep a pulse on how and what they're doing and what the issues are?

Then COVID happened. By that time, I was no longer with the company. They were legally forced to convert all their operations to remote almost overnight and for several months. Because everyone was forced to acclimate to remote work, the leadership team realized that with the right metrics, accountability, and meeting structure, they found ways to keep a pulse on what people were doing and stay abreast of their issues. They also discovered that without the distractions of coming to the office and all the hanging out around the proverbial water cooler, people, including the leadership team itself, became even more productive than they had been before.

When the lockdowns lifted and work with safety measures and social distancing became possible, this same leadership team who previously would not even consider a remote-work experiment decided to make almost the entire company, including leadership, remote and virtual indefinitely.

The same thing applies for FLs. They are experienced with virtual engagements and can preempt most fears around virtual FLs' lack of being in touch using regular check-ins, some probing questions, and collaborative tools such as Zoom, Slack, a good CRM, a good cloud-based project management system like Asana or Trello, and Google Docs or Sheets.

I admit that in-person human connection is irreplaceable. Many organizations and leaders feel, even after begrudgingly accepting remote work while it was an absolute necessity, that virtual work feels wrong to them. They have to make a cost-benefit analysis. If they can find a local FL who's a great fit for them, awesome! If not, they must ask whether the cost of remaining without that experienced leadership exceeds the downsides of a virtual FL.

It's not just certain business owners and leaders who strongly prefer in-person engagements; some FLs do as well. Brad Martyn founded FocusCFO twenty years ago in Columbus, Ohio. Today, FocusCFO has over one hundred associates and serves an area in the eastern United States stretching from Michigan to the north, Indiana to the west, Pennsylvania to the east, and south through the southeastern US states. Although their coverage is wide, Brad explained to me that one of the things that sets them apart is the depth of their belief that for an FCFO to be effective, they need to be physically on-site, or "embedded" within their clients. They find when a CFO only works with a company remotely, it is much harder to get a firm grasp on the people, the culture, and the real issues facing the business.

There is no wrong answer. The key is to be honest with yourself. If you believe the cost to you and your unique business of engaging with a virtual FL do exceed the benefit, it is probably not a good idea to convince yourself otherwise. The engagement will likely end in failure and profound frustration.

Time Commitment

FLs make three primary types of time commitments: X number of (i) days, (ii) half days, or (iii) hours per measuring period—that is, week or month. Some engagements even involve as much as half-time work; these individuals take on no more than one or two clients. Other FLs work with their clients only one or two hours per week or a half day per month.[20]

You must agree with your FL on expectations when it comes to time commitment because you can't define the accountabilities or deliverables without knowing how much time the FL has to accomplish them. As Gary Braun, owner of the FCSO firm Pivotal Advisors, says, you cannot expect your one-day-per-week FL to attend five meetings and still have time left over to create sales processes and manage a sales team.[21]

You should also discuss with potential FLs their client load in general relative to his or her proposed time commitment. Mark O'Donnell, Visionary (CEO) at EOS Worldwide, cautions against entering into an engagement when the FL's client capacity is filled to the max. As business ebbs and flows or an FL successfully enables you to grow, your needs may change. "It's set up for failure systemically when they have three to seven clients [if each are ten to fifteen hours per week]. They end up being forced to not do the right thing for one or

---

20 There are other types of executives who provide full-time, interim leadership during a time of transition or to effect a turnaround. That is not the subject of this book, but if this is what you need, I recommend that you visit www.InterimExecs.com, founded by Robert Jordan and Olivia Wagner, to learn more about this model and to find a great interim executive if that is the right fit for you.

21 "How to Vastly Improve Your Salespeople and Processes: Gary Braun Interview," *Win Win—An Entrepreneurial Community* podcast, episode 8, July 17, 2019, https://podcasts.apple.com/us/podcast/008-how-to-vastly-improve-your-sales-people-processes/id1465488607?i=1000444684443.

more of their clients based on a nonlinear growth trajectory of all their clients."

Another time-related factor is the fact that like everyone else, FLs need and want to take vacation from time to time. If they commit to a certain number of hours per week and a monthly retainer, they build in a mechanism for vacation time in their engagements.

Personally, as an FI, I give clients a reasonable amount of notice that I will be on vacation a certain week and then make up my day with them a different week. Other FLs simply never take vacation—they work remotely while the rest of their family enjoys the time away. I personally cannot endorse this approach, and most business owners understand the importance of taking time off and enjoying one's family, and recognize that in the end, this makes the people with whom they work more effective.

Cost

Many FLs charge a monthly retainer in exchange for a weekly or monthly time commitment. Some charge for each quarter in advance. And still others charge by the hour. Rates vary greatly depending on a number of factors:

- The time commitment

- The depth of the FL's experience

- Whether the FL is an independent solo practitioner or using a licensed system (licensees generally charge higher rates than solo practitioners)

- Whether the FL is part of an Organizational Fractional Leader firm (OFL) (OFLs generally charge more than both licensees and independent solo FLs)

- The local or regional market (FLs in major metropolitan areas charge more than an equivalent person outside a metro area)

Because of the extreme variation in the size and type of companies, FLs' experience level, and market rates in each geography, monthly retainer amounts vary significantly. It is therefore impossible to identify a narrow market rate for each type of FL.

Some FLs charge $2,000 for a half day per month or for one hour per week. Others charge $2,500 for a half day per week. Most charge $4,000 or $12,000 per month for a one-day-per-week commitment. I even know of some FLs whose clients pay about $15,000 per month for a one-day-per-week commitment.

Among those who charge an hourly fee, I have seen anywhere between $125 and $325 per hour. Some, both business owners and FLs, prefer the hourly model. Even though the hourly approach offers significant flexibility, it has several disadvantages:

- Hourly rates can do a disservice to business owners because it causes them to think twice before calling up their FL. It becomes like calling their lawyer—something they only do when absolutely necessary. This may result in underutilizing the FL's expertise since they may not know in advance the value they will get from talking decisions over with their FL.

- Hourly is often more expensive. FLs with an hourly rate counterbalance the risk they assume by not receiving a monthly commitment from their clients by charging more per hour than they would if they had been on retainer. Hourly rates can also be more expensive because they incentivize people to work more slowly.

- Hourly rates also have the potential to misalign business owners' and FLs' incentives by placing the focus on time spent rather than results obtained.

Some FLs agree on a hybrid retainer/hourly approach with clients by establishing a retainer for X number of hours per week beyond which the FL will bill the client at an agreed-upon hourly rate.

Another approach some FLs take is accepting a lower retainer in exchange for an equity interest. Cory Warfield, founder, C-level executive, and board member at multiple companies, says, "I find that when a company can get a Fractional Leader at the right time, he or she gets some shares and the shares are worth something. They incentivize the right Fractional Leader to come in and have some skin in the game." The typical arrangement Cory has seen is that the business owner pays the FL about half of his or her typical retainer and gives the other half of the retainer in the form of equity based on its value either at the beginning or end of the engagement.

Cross-Market Rates in a Virtual World

Another interesting dynamic that impacts FL rates is the increasingly borderless marketplace. Monthly retainers are generally lower for FLs living in smaller metropolitan and rural areas.

However, modern technology and the growing acceptance of remote work, particularly post-COVID, allows people to serve clients in larger cities on a virtual basis, thus potentially undercutting FLs in the same or similar markets as the business owners. This development has the potential to drive down market rates, which may benefit business owners and hurt FLs in those markets.

But there are a couple of wrinkles. One is in-person Fractional Leadership. Business owners who prefer to work with an FL in person obviously are not in competition with FLs living in markets with a lower cost of living.

Another wrinkle is workstyle. Although everyone is an individual, there are regional and local trends. Business owners often find that FLs in the same or a similar market have a common communication and workstyle. In New York, where I live, most business owners usually expect the people they work with to respond to communications quickly and get straight to the point. Be nice but no fluff. FLs in markets with different expectations about the pace or style of communication (e.g., easygoing, no-rush cultures) may put off or frustrate business owners whose workstyles do not align. For example, Jill Young, a Certified EOS Implementer in the Dallas-Fort Worth area and Head Coach at EOS Worldwide, told me that while she typically celebrates her clients' achievements of quarterly goals with something fun like an impromptu dance party, this does not fly with New York entrepreneurs.

Smaller markets naturally tend to have fewer FLs, which means there are fewer of them to bring down the market for those in larger metropolitan areas. Accordingly, to the extent

FLs find themselves competing with one another, most of the people they're competing against come from markets similar to their own. This creates an incentive to raise their own rates to something closer to the rates prevalent in the larger markets.

As markets bleed more and more into one another with the remote work revolution, a national or international market is beginning to develop, evening out the previously wider gaps between urban and rural markets.

Payment Terms

Many FLs, like myself, require clients to pay for each half month in advance, on the first and fifteenth of each month. I personally offer a money-back guarantee on the payment for the first half month if the client and I realize that we are not a good fit.

Others require a whole month in advance. And some require payment for each quarter in advance to take their clients' minds off money and onto the work they should be doing together since the fees are already paid.

Length of Engagement

Engagement lengths vary from just one quarter to years-long. There is no typical amount of time because the reasons business owners retain an FL vary so significantly.

Those who lose a full-time member of the leadership team or who are just beginning a search process may retain an FL as an interim solution during the process. Such engagements may last only three to six months and end with the successful transition to the FL's full-time replacement.

Other business owners retain fractional talent because they need an FL's expertise and leadership but cannot yet afford someone full-time. Engagements like this often last one to two years or longer. They end when businesses' finances and operations start to require full-time focus and commitment. Once they've onboarded the right person, usually with the FL's help, the FL can help with the transition and step out of the way.

I have personally had engagements of both types. I've worked for just six months, at the end of which I helped find my full-time replacement and transition them into the job. I've also worked for over a year and a half for the same client because that is what they needed and wanted.

Working Themselves Out of a Job

Mark O'Donnell, Visionary (CEO) at EOS Worldwide, whose EOS Implementers work with over 10,000 companies across the world, explained his view on the topic to me this way:

> It works great when the Fractional Leader comes in, puts all the processes in place, hires the ideal team the business needs, and then hires their own replacement. I know one Fractional Integrator who recently came into an $18 million service business, put the systems in place, hired other members of the leadership team, helped them hire a full-time Integrator, and then got out when they were a $30 million company. It was a great year-and-a-half bridge. It fails when the Fractional Leader or business owner wants to turn it into a long-term, permanent gig.

The purpose of an FL's service to their clients is to work themselves out of a job. Whether they join a company as an interim FL during a search process or because a client needs their expertise but cannot afford a full-time leader yet, the goal is usually to help their clients become independent of them and then smoothly and successfully transition them to a full-time executive.

FLs very often lead, or at least participate in, the process of searching for their replacement because they know better than anyone what the right candidate looks like. There is no one more qualified to find a CMO than another CMO and no one better to help select a CFO than another CFO. They know what to look for in ways business owners usually don't. The FLs help with drafting or commenting on a job description, supervising a recruiter's efforts, and interviewing and evaluating finalists to help the organization ensure it picks the right person. For example, I routinely interview my potential replacements in full-time Integrator (COO) searches for my clients, help with the selection process, and then transition the new hire into the role.

Some of the clients retaining Gershon Morgulis's FCFO firm, Imperial Advisory, use the FCFO to level up their financial systems and controls while training and mentoring an existing inexperienced CFO. Imperial Advisory FCFOs consider their engagements with these clients successfully concluded when they have trained their client's existing CFO to adequately fill their seat.

It may feel like there is a conflict of interest in this dynamic. How can someone honestly participate in a process that will cause their engagement to end?

The key to understanding this is understanding why FLs "go fractional." Most thrive on the novelty of new challenges, learning new industries, and working with new companies. They get bored with repetitive work. When they've leveled up a business's operations to the point that they no longer make ongoing substantive changes in the organization, they start to get bored. It's in the FL's interest, as much as their clients', to move on when they've made all the revolutionary changes their clients needed.

It's also critical to ensure both you and your FL are very clear from the beginning how long the engagement should last, that success must include finding the right full-time replacement, and what role the FL should have in that process. No one wants to end an engagement in failure. If you and the FL are clear when the relationship starts that success means finding a full-time replacement, this ameliorates any potential conflict of interest.

Strategic versus Tactical Leadership

FLs become part of your leadership team. They typically participate in leadership team meetings and decisions, create metrics for their direct reports, lead departmental meetings, drive accountability of their team's achievement of their goals, and coach and mentor team members. The high-level, strategic nature of most FLs' roles is critical because their primary value to you is their experience, leadership, and ability to drive your team's achievement of your desired results.

But don't full-time operations leaders, like COOs, drive day-to-day operations, such as ensuring deliveries or service calls happen on time, product deliveries are correct and timely, or that customers are satisfied at all times? How can someone do that on a fractional basis?

To understand the answer to this question, it's important to distinguish between someone's role as COO and another operations hat they might wear.

For instance, full-time COOs in smaller organizations often have two roles. The leadership, management, and accountability aspect of the COO role usually consumes about 20 percent of their bandwidth. But they also wear one or more *other* hats, such as director of operations or high-level project manager. This part of their job takes 80 percent of their time.

Business owners who engage an FCOO or FI, by contrast, split the COO role away from the project manager or head of operations role. They take that 20 percent bandwidth needed for the leadership/management/accountability part of the job and assign that to an FCOO or FI. They give the head of operations or project management responsibilities to someone else or several other people.

A $50 million healthcare staffing business asked Gershon Morgulis from Imperial Advisory to provide them with an FCFO. The person he placed joined them in their office one day each week. He used the in-depth knowledge and insight gained by becoming part of the company to give them strategic advice they could never have had otherwise, including how to invest in administrative tools to lower their overhead, what kind of new debt to incur, how to integrate an acquired business into their operations, formulate a sales commission structure, and prepare their CEO to wow their investors.

Imperial Advisory's FCFO could not have achieved all of this for the client if he had to personally do all of the day-to-day bookkeeping, A/R, A/P, and payroll. He supervised such people or teams but did not do that work himself. Substantive, front-line-type work takes away from FLs' main value proposition.

I hope I've convinced you not to undervalue the deeper and more powerful change an FL can make in your business at the level of leadership, management, and accountability when they are not distracted by also having the role of being a higher-level worker bee.

With that being said, some smaller companies in particular—that is, those in the five-to-twenty-person size range—sometimes need their FLs to provide both leadership and another set of hands at a higher level than the other members of their team can provide. Particularly with respect to FCOOs and FIs, there is a subset of companies and FLs who need and want to play a tactical as well as strategic role. I call these Doer Leaders versus Manager Leaders. I'll explain more about the Doer versus Manager distinction in Chapters 8 and 9, which cover FLs who focus on operations.

Organizational Fractional Leadership Providers

There are two primary categories of FLs: OFLs and independent FLs. There are some differences between them and no one model is right for everyone. You must therefore consider which kind you want or whether you're open to both.

OFLs are organizations who assign individual FLs to clients. They either hire these individual FLs directly, make them partners, or enter into independent contractor relationships with them. In this model, you pay the OFL and the OFL pays the individual FL. This model has several advantages, each of which are discussed below: (1) accountability, (2) standardization, and (3) peer learning.

Accountability. The OFL takes responsibility for the services provided by the individual FL. If there are any issues, you can approach the company to help resolve the problem. If the initial FL does not work out, they can provide you with a replacement or supplement their abilities with those of someone else on the team with a complementary skillset. This saves you from the need to start over at square one searching for someone else.

Standardization. OFLs usually create a standardized service model—that is, some proven process they have found effective. All the FLs on their team use this proven process. In this sense, working with an OFL is more like staying at a Hilton or Holiday Inn rather than an independent hotel. The different substantive types of Fractional Leadership (CMOs, CFOs, etc.) have no governing body or accrediting organization, so using an OFL is one way of going through a standardized process to achieve your desired end result.

Peer Learning. Finally, FLs serving clients through an OFL are part of a team with a wide variety of backgrounds and experiences. Some OFLs hold weekly virtual meetings where a group of FLs shares the issues they're facing with clients. Those who have encountered a similar situation offer guidance. This helps clients by leveraging multiple FLs' knowledge and perspectives to solve their problems.

Independent Fractional Leaders

There are factors that mitigate in favor of working with a solo practitioner independent FL rather than an OFL for some business owners: (1) price, (2) independence, and (3) customization.

Price. The first advantage of working with an independent FL is price. OFLs are typically more expensive than their "single shingle" counterparts, sometimes by as much as double. For many business owners, this factor alone is determinative because they cannot afford some OFLs' rates for the time commitment they believe they need.

Independence. Some business owners prefer working with an independent FL because their personal hardwiring makes them more comfortable with independent operators. They see themselves as independent, entrepreneurial, and one-of-a-kind and therefore seek out FLs who share that vibe. They want to work with people who can fully define the engagement. Such people bristle at anything that feels overly corporate, and some OFLs come across that way to them.

Customization. Finally, some business owners look for a customized engagement and see OFLs' standardization as a bad fit. They want their FL to custom-tailor his or her services and methods to their business's unique needs. Although most OFLs custom-tailor each engagement to fit exactly what their clients need, some perceive them as too cookie-cutter for their tastes.

Regardless of whether you decide that an OFL or an independent FL is a better fit for you and your business ,you'll leverage the benefit of someone with years of experience at multiple companies to guide you to accomplish what you could not on your own.

Fully Independent versus Licensee Fractional Leaders

Among independent FLs, there are two subtypes: those who work fully on their own and licensees or franchisees of a standardized system. Examples of the latter include FCSOs who use the Sales Xceleration or SalesQB frameworks.

Some people prefer fully independent FLs. They see no need for the "unnecessary complication" of an outside system if the FL has experience, knowledge, and strong references. They do not want to spend time, money, or energy on parts of a system that don't really apply to them simply because they are part of "the package."

On the other hand, licensed systems provide a proven process. Some business owners want their FL to use a system that works for thousands of organizations and has been implemented by dozens or hundreds of FLs. They need and want results as soon as possible. They're hiring an FL because they know they themselves are not experts in the field and recognize that their perception that part of a system is unnecessary may be unfounded.

Licensed FLs also bring technological tools with them engineered specifically for their clients' goals. This saves the need for custom software or web app development and facilitates faster implementation custom-designed for business owners' needs.

How Fractional Leaders Structure Engagements to Negate Potential Pitfalls

Many people are hesitant to make the leap to use Fractional Leadership. How can someone understand the business if they're not there full-time? How can someone drive accountability and results in a team they hardly see? How can someone be part of your leadership team when they're not physically there? The next two subsections will answer these questions.

Understanding the Business When They're Not There Full-Time

How can FLs understand your business well enough to effectively act as a member of the leadership team when they're not there full-time? Why are they no better than the "drive-by consultants" we spoke about who do their best to meet with as many people as they can to get a good understanding of the company but who, through no fault of their own, rarely *get* it?

The difference is that FLs embed themselves with your company, whether they're with you physically or virtually. FLs aren't drive-by consultants because they become *part of* your leadership team. They collaborate with the other members of the leadership team on a consistent basis and work, week in, week out (or month in, month out) with the team or function they lead. They get to know your business, people, and culture over the months or years you work with them.

They do not simply state their opinion after an investigation. They do not supplant your team's culture, your knowledge of your market, and your experience. Rather, they use what they know works from past experience to focus and concretely implement the knowledge you and your people already possess through a far more effective execution than you had before.

Let's make this more concrete. I began working with a wood flooring installer as their FI. Two of the members of the leadership team had quarterly goals related to documenting certain core processes that were unclear and inconsistently applied at the time. This caused tremendous frustration. One process related to collecting A/R and the other had to do with how to install certain types of flooring most effectively.

I'm not a flooring expert. I'll just put that out there at the outset. It doesn't matter. I'm good at documenting processes and figuring out the best way to create accountability around executing those processes. I don't need to understand the nuances of flooring installation to channel the knowledge of the head of operations into a short, two-page process document. I showed him how to implement a couple of simple metrics to ensure that once the operations team was trained on that process, they were held accountable to execute the process the right way, every time.

When the Cat's Away...

How do you ensure that the members of the team don't fall back into old habits and do things the way they'd become ingrained to during the 80 percent of the time the FL isn't around?

This is a great question, and it has a simple answer. FLs know from experience that you don't create effective teams and core functions of the business by hovering over people to ensure they do things right. In startup mode, business owners want to make sure that every part of their new company is working well, so they hover; many business owners and leadership team members simply assume that's how it works in larger companies, just on a larger scale with more managers overlooking more people's work. But that's not the best way to get results.

FLs create effective teams by creating accountable teams who don't need a helicopter manager. They do that by first ensuring that the team is made up of the right people who share the workstyle and core values of the company. Next, they define the team's process and set weekly metrics and goals which track those processes to create accountability around execution. That's it.

Let's say you retain an FCSO who puts in place a new sales process and implements a CRM to create visibility, accountability, and reporting around sales. He or she creates metrics in the company's chosen CRM for leads entered, outgoing emails sent, demo calls conducted, and sales closed, each with a specific minimum threshold to be considered on-track. If someone on the team doesn't use the CRM to enter leads or send outgoing emails or log demo calls, then they won't make the numbers to which they are held accountable at the weekly sales meeting with the FCSO. It's that simple.

FLs don't have to be physically with the team all the time as long as they set up a system of accountability and hold people to that system. They train, answer questions, mentor, and perhaps sit in on calls or listen to recordings during the time they're with the team, thus driving effective execution without needing to be there full-time.

Next

You now understand what Fractional Leadership is, the kinds of blockages it breaks through for business owners, and how it works at a high level. The next question is whether it is right for you and your unique business. In the next chapter, I walk you through five questions to help you determine whether you're a candidate for Fractional Leadership. I discuss several alternatives if the answer is no. I also teach a method to help you determine which kind of FL you need (i.e., marketing, sales, operations, finance, or technology). Spoiler alert: it's not always the kind you thought.

4.

How to Figure Out Whether You're a Candidate for Fractional Leadership

NOW YOU UNDERSTAND WHAT FRACTIONAL LEADERSHIP is and how bringing on an FL can fast-track your business past the ceilings you're slamming your head against. You may now realize that you need an FL in your business.

I've seen five main areas where business owners discover that Fractional Leadership is not a good fit for them .Below are five questions that will help you determine whether you're ready to retain an FL and an explanation of each one.

Five Questions to Determine Whether Fractional Leadership Is a Good Fit

1. Are you looking for (a) leadership, strategy, management, and someone to drive accountability? Or (b) someone who can personally get a lot of stuff done?

The main value of Fractional Leadership is bringing experienced, been-there-done-that direction into your leadership team to collaboratively lead and drive execution by creating discipline and accountability around a certain core function of your business.

If what you need is primarily someone to personally get things done, then Fractional Leadership may not be right for you.

Instead, you might need to hire a manager-level person, elevate someone to a greater level of responsibility, or you may have the wrong person in a key role. If that person happens to be a family member, it creates a thorny issue.[22] You may be tempted to retain an FL to escape having to make a difficult change with one or more of your people in hopes that the FL will "whip them into shape." Unfortunately, the only solution to people issues is either helping them level up or replacing them with someone more suited to the role. Retaining an FL does immunize you from the need to make a change when you have wrong-person or wrong-seat issues.[23] It simply costs more and delays the inevitable.

That being said, particularly with respect to operations, I have found that some smaller companies (usually those with five to twenty employees) match up well with FLs with experience at similar-sized businesses. In these engagements, the FL has a dual role of acting as a member of the leadership team as well as just getting stuff done. I call these Doer Leaders. Particularly for operations, there is sometimes a place for a dual head of operations and FCOO role, but it's a tricky balance and you must ensure that your expectations

---

22 For more detail on how to handle the particularly thorny issue of working with family members, see "How to Succeed at Growing a Family Business: Sara Stern Interview," *Win Win—An Entrepreneurial Community* podcast, episode 7, July 7, 2019, https://podcasts.apple.com/us/podcast/007-how-to-succeed-at-growing-family-business-sara/id1465488607?i=1000444161873.

23 Although having a great FL does not mean you don't have to let go someone who isn't performing, FLs are often great at helping drive efforts to level people up or help move them out and bring in people who are a better fit and perform the way the business needs.

are aligned with those of your potential FL. I'll explain more about this in Chapters 8 and 9.

For example, Rachel Beider, founder and CEO of Press Modern Massage and author of *Massage MBA*, worked to scale a massage practice in Brooklyn, New York. She fought tooth and nail over about seven years to expand into seventeen treatment rooms in two locations.

But she was stressed out, overwhelmed, and anxious all the time. Everything was on her head. She had to supervise her staff, drive expansion to new locations, furnish the treatment rooms, lead marketing, and oversee everything else that went into running a business. She felt like it was actually running her into the ground. Rachel could not afford a full-time COO, so she finally connected with another woman who could act as her FCOO to take over supervision of the staff and execute on the various physical expansions. That way, Rachel could focus more on building the business, marketing, and clinical supervision and culture, things she loved doing and was great at. She credits her FCOO with restoring her sanity and her ability to expand her practice to five locations in less than a third of the time it took her to open just her second location.

For those who need more of a Doer Leader, there are two main approaches they can take:

- Hire a manager or head of operations full-time. They don't have to be super experienced in larger companies or be leadership team material. Business owners considering this route should understand that such a manager-level or head of operations will still cost more than the people they already have on board. Once they have a manager-level person on the team, they can then reconsider Fractional Leadership because the FL will then have someone they can rely on to drive day-to-day tactical execution while the FL brings greater strategic and accountability leadership.

- Find an FI or FCOO who's looking for a more tactical, Doer Leader role in addition to the leadership element. I know many such people available and I usually introduce those business owners to two or three of them whom I can vouch for.

In my experience, Doer Leaders are a relatively small part of the Fractional Leadership community because they work more hours for a smaller number of clients. Whenever I speak with potential clients, I always probe for a clear understanding of their expectations so I know if they're looking for an FI more focused on leading, managing, and creating accountability (a Manager Leader), or if they're looking more for a tactical, get-'er-done, head of operations (a Doer Leader). For those business owners who are looking for a Doer Leader, I let them know that I am more of the leadership, management, and accountability type of FL and that I'm probably not a good fit for what they're looking for.

For most business owners, the right time for Fractional Leadership is when they desperately need the experience, leadership, and ability to drive execution and accountability—that is, a Manager Leader. Fractional Leadership is usually not right for people who just need an extra set of hands.

2. Do you (a) already have one or more members of your leadership team participating remotely? Or (b) is there a strong culture of the leadership team being physically together in one office all of the time?

Many FLs work in-person with their clients. But with a whole world of businesses and FLs living far from the businesses who need them, the likelihood is that your perfect FL puzzle piece may not live in your geographic area. This question is apropos to that scenario.

If your entire leadership team, or even one other member of it, already works remotely, this is a good sign that you can effectively work with an FL remotely.

I've found that business owners whose entire leadership team physically meets and works together at one location are much less likely to be open to working with a remote FL. When the entire leadership team sits together in one meeting room and only the FL, who is not even with the business full-time, participates remotely, most of the time, unless they are the clear leader of the meeting, they will be and feel left out.

Even if the remote FL is the clear meeting leader, awkward conversations, interruptions, and overtalking inevitably take place. That is acceptable for one-off meetings here and there, but it usually doesn't work well with leadership teams who must collaborate and meet on a regular basis. The nightmare of hybrid meetings usually involves sidebar conversations between the people who are together in-person. Whoever is remote ends up feeling left out.

Bill Stratton, a Professional EOS Implementer® in Lancaster, Pennsylvania, advises against hybrid in-person/remote meetings. If even one member of the leadership team participates remotely in a meeting, everyone should participate remotely. If you avoid hybrid meetings by holding them online even if several people are in the same office, then everyone is on a level playing field, so to speak. This framework is usually much more successful. If you value each member's presence in the meeting and there's a reason why they're there, then it's worth it to forgo the benefit of in-person interaction for a portion of the team in favor of full engagement by the entire leadership team, whether this includes FLs or not.

It is critical that you be honest with yourself about your organization's culture. If you cannot find a local FL and you value in-person, physical interaction above the practical benefits of a virtual FL, then Fractional Leadership is probably not right for you.

But if you already have one or more members of your leadership team participating remotely, or knowing yourself, you believe that you are ready, willing, and able to work remotely with an FL, then you may be a candidate for Fractional Leadership.

3. Are you someone who (a) can get comfortable trusting and listening to an experienced, knowledgeable executive who's not in your business full-time? Or (b) do you know you'll never be able to trust, listen to, or respect the opinion and guidance of someone who is not there full-time?

Colonel Johann Gottlieb Rall was commander of the German-Hessian mercenary army hired by the British to help them put down the American Revolution. He was charged with defending Trenton, New Jersey from the rebels.

Although the Hessians did not know it at the time, General Washington was leading his freezing militia army across the Delaware River to attack the British position in Trenton that cold, rainy night after Christmas 1776. On his way to dinner that evening, someone gave Rall a note containing intelligence from a British spy within the revolutionaries' ranks warning of the impending attack by Washington's army the next morning.

Because Rall held the revolutionaries in such disdain, he blew off the warning. He dismissively placed the note in his jacket pocket and went on to enjoy his dinner. Rall and his troops celebrated the holiday in the main barracks that night or in local Trentonian homes abandoned because of the occupation. Rall himself dined well and got drunk that evening after enjoying a convivial game of checkers.

Washington's attack the following morning, December 26, was devastating. It turned the tide of the Patriots' then-unbroken losing streak in the early days of the Revolutionary War. In the ensuing battle, Colonel Rall himself was shot twice in the side and ultimately died of his wounds, with the note warning of the attack still in his pocket.

Some people are simply wired to trust only themselves or other insiders. They approach business with a full-time-or-bust mindset. "If you're not all-in, you aren't committed and can't or just won't *get it*." Others recognize the value outside experts' experience can give them. They know that like the spy's intelligence about Washington's attack given to Colonel Rall, outside expertise is often the critical difference between success and failure.

I have asked other FLs to tell me about times when an engagement ended badly. I find we can learn more from failure than we can from success. The most common examples were variations on this theme. The business owners were unhappy with how things were going but dismissed the advice of outsiders, no matter how attentive and experienced they were.

Good FLs know that you, as the owner, and your team know your business better than any outsider. They take this into account and expertly marry their own experience to your knowledge of your business and market to create and drive the most effective path.

Some people intellectually know this is true but are hardwired to distrust outsiders. If this is you, it is neither right nor wrong. It is simply true. And to repress that knowledge and retain an FL despite your preferences will simply cause the engagement to end in frustration and failure for both sides.

4. Will you, as the business owner, (a) truly commit to reinforce the FL's role and any new processes or procedures with their team? Or (b) will you often allow circumvention of the new processes or procedures or initiate or allow end runs around the FL?

Let's talk about end runs. *Merriam-Webster* defines an end run as "a secret or dishonest attempt to avoid a rule, problem, etc." In the business context, Gino Wickman and Mark C. Winters define it in *Rocket Fuel: The One Essential Combination That Will Get You More of What You Want from Your Business* as "when an employee goes around a manager to complain or get a better/different answer to his problem." It is also an end run when a CEO or owner directly approaches an executive's or manager's direct reports to circumvent an agreed-upon process, hierarchy, or decision.

George R. R. Martin said, "Most men would rather deny a hard truth than face it." Know thyself. If you know when you bring in an FL that you won't be able to stop yourself from undermining the systems, standards, changes, and processes you asked them to establish for you, then Fractional Leadership is probably not for you. If you won't have your FL's back, don't bring an FL into the business.

Successful leaders endeavor to reinforce the authority, processes, and standards set by their trusted executives and managers. This means redirecting attempted end runs by employees or vendors to the appropriate executive. It also means not instigating end runs. It is critical to talk with potential FLs about how you and they will navigate the unique challenges of a fractional engagement to avoid end runs when you're in the business full-time and they are not.

It goes without saying that having your FL's back and not entertaining or instigating end runs only works if you have trust. That is the foundation of every successful Fractional Leadership engagement. And you can only trust your FL if he or she is the "right person" (shares your core values and culture) and is in the right seat (understands their role, wants it, and has the skills and experience to excel at it). If any of those elements are missing, the relationship is not going to work.

I discuss in the next chapter how to not only find the right FL for you but also ensure that they are the "right person" in the "right seat" before pulling the trigger with them.

5. Can you (a) afford 20–50 percent of the cost of an experienced full-time executive? Or (b) is that more than you can afford?

This question is related to the first question—whether you need someone to lead, manage, and create systems for accountability, or someone to *personally* get stuff done. FLs' main value proposition is their experience and leadership, not merely as highly skilled technicians. And Fractional Leadership is far more affordable than hiring the right person full-time. But it is only an option if you can responsibly afford it. So how much does a good FL charge?

To engage an FL for far less commitment, cost, and ramp-up time than a similarly experienced full-time executive, you can expect to pay, for the same time commitment, about double the hourly or monthly cost of what you'd pay a full-time employee if you converted their compensation to hourly.

What does that mean practically speaking?

Let's assume a full-time experienced CXO in your market would command approximately $220,000 in base compensation, a $30,000 bonus, about $20,000 in noncash benefits, and an additional 12 percent in taxes and other insurance ($26,400). That's a total of $296,400 annually. That's almost $25,000 per month. Using the aforementioned "2 to 1" time commitment rule of thumb, you can expect to pay a similar FL about $10,000 per month (give or take) for about a day-per-week of time. That's 34 percent of what it would cost to hire someone of their caliber full-time.

Let us imagine that this sounds like too much and you want to pay around $4,000 per month. That is the rate you'd pay for someone who, if you hired them full-time, about

$100,000. If you probably can't realistically find an executive with deep enough experience for $100,000, then you probably won't get an equivalent FL for $4,000 per month for a day per week. If you can find a C-level leader in your market for $100,000, then $4,000 per month may be the right amount if there is someone available in your market.

Can you afford a great FL? If so, great! If not, you may not be ready for Fractional Leadership right now.

What should you do if you cannot afford to retain an FL or you're not a candidate for Fractional Leadership because of your answers to questions one to four? You have several options. The next part of this chapter walks you through several alternatives available to you.

Your Options if You Aren't a Candidate for Fractional Leadership

Let's say you answered "(b)" more often than "(a)" to the above five questions. Fractional Leadership isn't a great fit for you. That doesn't take away the gap in your or your team's knowledge and experience that's holding you back. You're caught in the grip of the Entrepreneurial Catch-22, but Fractional Leadership isn't an option for some reason. What do you do now?

Here are your main options.

Wait until you can afford full-time: Continue growing slowly the way you have been until now. It may mean a couple more years of tortuous and painful growth (i.e., more of what you're already going through). Your circumstances may not allow for any other option. Keep plugging away, and at some point, you'll scale big enough to afford an FL or to hire the kind of experienced executive you need full-time.

Find the money and hire full-time right now: If you don't want to forgo the benefit of having someone with knowledge and experience full-time, you may want to invest, raise (i.e., give up equity), or borrow enough money to hire someone full-time right now even though the role isn't quite ready for full-time yet. This may entail asking the person to take on some other role in the interim or paying them for a role the company hasn't quite grown into yet while your operations grow to match the person you've hired.

Hire a manager-level person: I also mentioned this option in my explanation of the first of the five questions above. Consider expanding the depth of your bench before you bring on a full-time executive or even an FL. This is often the best bet particularly if you're a smaller company (five to twenty people) and/or cannot afford an experienced FL's rates.

Go the consultant route: I spoke tongue-in-cheek about "drive-by consultants" above. One of the things that make these engagements challenging is that they require a lot of time on your or one of your leadership team member's part to work with the consultant and then drive execution of whatever solutions they propose or assist with.

If you or one of your people can't devote the significant time necessary to oversee and then implement the work done by the consultant, you need to find a way around this lack of bandwidth. You must do an analysis of how you're spending your time. Identify the lower-level or more administrative tasks that eat up a lot of your time and then hire or delegate one or more people to take over those tasks to open up more bandwidth so you can run with the solutions proposed by your chosen consultant.[24]

How to Figure Out Which Type of Fractional Leader You Need

Let's assume you've determined that you are a candidate for Fractional Leadership. You may even have a very good idea of what kind of FL you need, whether in marketing, sales, operations, finance, or technology. But I encourage you to ask yourself one last time what kind of FL you *really* need.

Why? Because sometimes people think they need one kind of help because they have a glaring symptom—let's say in technology—but in reality, it's just that, a symptom. Business owners very often know where they need the most help, and this usually indicates the kind of FL they should retain. But sometimes their first instinct is misleading.

Here's an example. Damon Neth, William Mince, and Jim Treleaven in *X-Formation: Transforming Business through Interim Executive Leadership* recount how an $8.5 million consumer products company hired an interim CIO to implement new systems because they thought their issue was with technology, not process, since they had already done significant work to improve their operations.

---

24 For more on delegation, if your company is running on EOS and you have an EOS Implementer, ask them about the Delegate and Elevate™ tool. For everyone else, please read the blog post by Gino Wickman, author of Traction, called "Business Leadership—5 Steps to Help You Delegate and Elevate," https://www.eosworldwide.com/blog/789-eos-business-leadership-steps-help-you-delegate-and-elevate.

Unfortunately, after the CIO began, he realized the issue was not technology but the organization's structure. Accountability for their operations was spread among three different people. The buck did not stop with one person, so in effect, no one was accountable. This led to inherently ineffective systems that could not be overcome by cosmetic process improvements. The company had to completely restructure to have any hope of scaling up.

Fortunately, the CIO had the knowledge and experience to lead this restructuring and systems optimization. Within three months, the same team began processing 100 percent more orders with 85 percent greater accuracy.

With the benefit of hindsight, should the consumer products seller have retained an interim COO or CEO? Perhaps. But they did not because they decided who they needed based on their assumption about the nature of the solution to their problem. In reality, the technological solution they thought they needed was based on a misdiagnosis of the underlying problem.

However, the ability to distinguish underlying causes and its symptoms is precisely why business owners retain experienced FLs. It's not always easy to figure out what you really need. To help you determine which kind of FL you need, I've developed a short two-question survey. I'll explain each question below.

1. What part of your business is your greatest pain point?

First, identify your business's greatest pain point:

- **Marketing.** Are you spending exorbitant amounts on "random acts of marketing"? Do you lack the data to make educated decisions about where and how you market and aren't sure how to collect or analyze that data? Do you lack a carefully crafted message and story to apply consistently throughout your marketing, sales, and customer retention cycles? If much of this describes you, you may need an FCMO.

- **Sales.** Do you lack a defined sales process? Does each salesperson do things their own way, with their own message, and with no consistency? Are sales and marketing misaligned? Did you promote your best salesperson to head of sales, but it's a disaster because that person is now no longer the superstar salesperson they used to be and stinks as a manager and leader? Do you spend most of your time half-managing or driving the sales team? Do you struggle with a lack of visibility into what specific activities drive the desired sales numbers or what salespeople's specific activities are? Did you hire an underqualified person to manage sales so you could spend less, but now you're suffering? If so, you may need an FCSO.

- **Operations.** Are your pain points spread throughout your operation or more people-oriented? Do your people suffer from confusion and uncertainty about the right accountabilities and structure for the organization? Do you lack a clearly understood and widely communicated vision for who you are and where your organization is going? Do you notice morale problems or disturbingly high and unwelcome turnover? Do people execute on your product or service offering inconsistently—that is, does it look different for each customer or client? Are your processes undocumented, trained in via oral tradition, and carried out unreliably, without discipline and accountability across the board? Do you lack the right forward-looking, activity-based data to spot and solve issues before they go from potential problems to past failures? If many of these issues describe you, you may need an FCOO or FI (for companies running on EOS).

- **Finance.** Do you lack expertise or oversight into expenses, collections, cash flow, rolling twelve-month budgeting, analysis of actual versus budgeted? Do you suspect that you are bleeding money, leaving it on the table, or hitting a desperate cash crunch but lack the internal expertise, experience, or time/bandwidth to take ownership of all of that? Are you about to acquire another company or are you considering being acquired and lack the financial experience to conduct the necessary due diligence and financial analysis? Are you fundraising and need more financial leadership? If some of these challenges describe you, you may need an FCFO.

- **Technology.** Do you rely on technological systems and platforms, whether proprietary or third party, for the very existence of the business or its core processes? Do you sell technology you've developed to your customers as your main product or products? Have you found that you lack anyone with the bandwidth or experience to set direction and manage risk? Do you have freelance or outsourced development teams but no expert to manage them robustly, properly hold them accountable, perform QA testing, and ensure the products they're building do what they are supposed to in an agreed-upon time frame? If so, you may need an FCIO or FCTO.

Now that you've identified which of the five major categories of Fractional Leadership represent your greatest pain point ,ask yourself the following question:

2. Is that the *underlying* problem or merely a symptom?

Stop for a moment. Ask yourself: To the best of your ability to know the answer, is your answer to the first question the real issue? Or is it actually a symptom of another problem?

Think about the consumer products company I wrote about above. They thought because they had worked to optimize their processes that lack of effective technology was their biggest problem, so they hired a CIO. In reality, their issue was the overall accountability structure in the organization.

One problem I've seen is a sales team persistently underperforming. You might be tempted to retain an FCSO to optimize the sales process, data, compensation, training, or incentives. But what if sagging sales is only the symptom of a marketing problem?

If the marketing process is delivering your sales team unqualified leads who don't need your product or service or who cannot afford your rates, then *of course* your sales team cannot close more deals. They must spend all their time qualifying leads. So in reality, this organization needs an FCMO more than an FCSO.

Approach friends or colleagues who have their own businesses, preferably ones bigger than yours. Speak with people in a peer advisory group like Vistage, Entrepreneurs' Organization, Young Professionals Organization, or The Alternative Board. Place the question before them and get outside, trusted feedback on what part of your business is the biggest underlying cause of you repeatedly hitting your head against the ceiling your business is hitting.

Next

Now that you understand what Fractional Leadership is, what it can do for you, whether you're a candidate, and what kind of FL you need, you may be wondering how on earth to find the right FL and how to know whether they're actually good and don't simply talk a good game.

In the next chapter, I will explain exactly how to find the right FL for you and the steps you need to take to ensure that the engagement achieves everything you want and need.

5.

How to Find the Right Fractional Leader for Maximum Impact

CYNDI GAVE, OWNER OF EMPLOYEE SELECTION, performance, and development firm The Metiss Group, says, "Part of the reason we brought on a fractional is because we can't imagine what a full-time one would actually do."[25]

Cyndi admits that she made some missteps in the past selecting FCMOs who were not the right fit for her. "I think the challenge was that if we're not clear about exactly what we want, they will provide what they're good at, which may not be what we need."

The Metiss Group needed a new website and rebrand, but the first FCMO she hired wanted to do SEO and a lot of related work for them. She admits that she didn't hold them accountable to do what she thought they really needed because "they're the experts." Plus, as it is with many of us, it's hard to have hard conversations.

---

25 "The Pinnacles and Pitfalls in Hiring a Fractional Leader for Your Organization: Interview with Cyndi Gave," *Win Win—An Entrepreneurial Community* podcast, episode 65, October 13, 2020, https://podcasts. apple.com/us/podcast/065-pinnacles-pitfalls-in-hiring-fractional-leader/ id1465488607?i=1000494589381.

The problem is that SEO did nothing for her business. Because The Metiss Group performs a service for their clients that is a little outside the box, there weren't any universally known keywords their potential clients tended to use. But that first FCMO continued insisting that it was important that they continue working on SEO.

Finally, Cyndi decided to sever the relationship and bring on another FCMO. This person had a public relations background. And even though that was not what she needed, it took spending another $12,000 with them to realize that this person was not a good fit either.

Cyndi began to wonder whether the kind of fractional marketing help she knew she needed even existed.

The more she thought about it, Cyndi realized that most of the company's revenue came from referrals who'd heard her speaking at various events. She had no systematic way of targeting her connectors who could refer her to more public speaking opportunities. And no one had reviewed her presentations to make sure they complemented her speeches and made the maximum impact.

Finally, she got very clear with herself on what she needed and communicated that to other FCMOs she spoke with. In the end, she found Jim Burris, owner of Burris Creative based in Charlotte, North Carolina. He listened to her thoughts, and once they were on the same page, he delivered exactly what she needed.

Drill Down on What You Need and Want

The first step is clarifying to yourself what specific accomplishments or deliverables you need to see from an FL and over what time frame. If you cannot clearly articulate this to yourself, you won't be able to communicate it to a potential FL. It is critical to communicate your expectations because if you don't clearly tell a potential FL what you need from them or if you leave things out that are important to you, it's going to lead to misunderstandings, disappointment, and potential failure.

Here are several factors to consider so you can narrow down your search.

Industry Experience

Depending on the kind of FL you're looking for, ask yourself (1) whether specific industry experience is very important to you (it's always a plus), and if so, (2) what particular kind of industry experience does the FL need to have. In some instances, industry expertise is critical and in some situations it is almost irrelevant.

Personally, in my work as an FI, my clients' industries have varied wildly, from healthcare, cybersecurity, multifamily real estate, and nonprofit to media, e-commerce, and construction. My familiarity or unfamiliarity with the substantive product or service they provided did not impede my success at all (in my humble estimation). Industry experience is less relevant for my clients because I provide them with leadership, structure, and management, and I create systems for accountability. I don't need to know how to install wood flooring to help a Head of Operations document a clear, concise process his or her people should follow to install wood flooring.

For some, however, it is not worthwhile to engage an FL without relevant industry experience because that knowledge is extremely relevant. The learning curve would be too great and take too long to overcome if they lack specific expertise in what they do. For example, I helped a cybersecurity client find an FCSO. Because their target market was government agencies and government contractors, the sales process and cycle differed markedly from the pure commercial market. We therefore limited our search to FCSOs with government contracting experience.

The Situational Experience You Need

If you need a dentist, you don't go to a doctor. And if you need your plumbing fixed, you don't go to a dentist.

You have a problem that's causing you to seek out an FL. Whether that's a financial crisis, an operational sticking point, or the fact that your supply of leads dried up once you used up your low-hanging-fruit prospects, you have something you need to get done. It's critical that you ask in advance whether your potential FL has that kind of experience.

If you need someone to build and drive a sales team to the desired results, ensure they've already created a sales process, metrics to hold people accountable, and staffed up a rock star sales team.

If you need to buy another company or sell yours, you want someone with M&A experience.

If you need help revamping your manufacturing process, you probably want someone who knows Lean Six Sigma or has other demonstrated manufacturing process improvement experience.

If you need to build a brand and launch a new product, you need an FCMO who's successfully overseen several product rollouts.

And if you need a CTO who's going to build a new product, you need to confirm they've built and iterated a new app or platform before.

Core Values

It may sound fluffy or like a nice-to-have, but core values make the difference between success and failure.

Although Fractional Leadership is a great tool, nothing works perfectly for every person all the time. I've asked a lot of people the biggest reason they say that any engagements have not worked out, and the number one, stand-out answer has been lack of core values fit.

Cory Warfield, founder, C-level executive, and board member at multiple companies, has used FLs in a number of his ventures. He told me that cultural fit is the number one reason he's seen those engagements not work out.

> Fractional Leaders need to accept a certain culture rather than change it. The temptation is to try to change it. When I see it work is when the leaders accept whatever the culture is. One of my startups, which had raised a couple million dollars and had about thirty employees, thought they wanted to run it like a Fortune 500 company. So when they retained a couple of FLs, they brought in executives who had led billion-dollar international brands. Rather than Google sheets, they need Smartsheets. Rather than a free version of Zoho, they're using HubSpot. They want to do everything in the corporate way, the most expensive way, unfortunately.

Later, Cory brought the former CTO at an education-based business into another one of his companies as FCTO. Because he had been in more of a bootstrapped, startup environment, he was "just a lot more fun. He was able to kind of work within the way that we were running that organization."

Shortly after the onset of COVID, like so many of us, Andrea Perales, founder of FI firm ACP Enlightening, was going through a difficult time and needed a client. She took someone on as a client even though she got a bad feeling about the owner throughout the three meetings they held before going forward. Because she needed the business at the time, she went into the engagement anyway.

Part of the problem was that this client needed her to act as his CFO because she had a finance background even though she no longer enjoyed that type of work. The other issue was that she has a very positive, optimistic nature whereas he was predisposed to think and speak negatively about everyone in his company, including her. She nevertheless did her best to deliver great results for him and the company.

After one explosive meeting with the owner, Andrea told him that it was in the company's and her own best interest for her to move on to another opportunity. She left after a three-week transition period. She could not have been happier. She summarized her takeaway from this painful engagement with this message: "When you feel like you do not have a connection, do not go forward! Sometimes you feel like you need it, but don't do it. Listen to your gut feelings. Do not work with someone if you don't feel a connection—if your core values are not aligned."

When I was first starting out as an FI, I asked Jill Young, Certified EOS Implementer and Head Coach at EOS

Worldwide, for her advice. What is the most important thing I should know to be a successful FI? Her advice was to ensure that I was a good core values fit with my clients.

What are core values? Great business authors like Patrick Lencioni and Jim Collins have spilled a lot of ink on this topic, so I'll simply summarize them by explaining that core values are the ways of acting and behaving that come from your core. You can't change them even if you wanted to. And you wouldn't act against those values even if continuing to follow them were not profitable or would drive you out of business.

One of my own core values is "straight talk." I don't have the skills or patience to think three steps ahead before I say something, be excessively tactful, or posture myself to make someone else think something was their own idea. I'm just not wired that way. Other people are very adept at this, but I am not.

My bluntness and straight-to-the-point communication style grate on some people. That's okay. Both business owners and FLs must know ourselves and get an initial impression of the other so we can avoid entering into a relationship with someone whom we'll hate working with and who will annoy us.

An internet advertising company owner I know, along with the rest of his leadership team, is very focused on winning, absolute accountability, and results. They attempted to retain an FCSO on retainer for about a day of work each week to level up the sales team. After just a couple of weeks, he found himself wondering how the FCSO was spending his time. The CEO asked around and found out that this individual would email team members for a sales call "ride-along" and simply wait for a response for weeks without taking ownership over making the meetings happen. Worst of all, he failed to communicate what he was doing or the challenges he was facing to the CEO. His laissez-faire style grated on the business owner. Extracting updates from him was like pulling teeth. Needless to say, the engagement ended quickly thereafter.

In all of these examples, the FL or business owner did not lack any substantive skills or experience. They were a mismatch in terms of essential workstyle—that is, core values.

How to Find Your Fractional Leader

The most common method is to search the internet. Although very manual and time-consuming, this is how it's been done until now. Search using terms like "fractional," "outsourced," and whatever kind of C-level position you're looking to fill. If you need the person to be local, add in the name of your city.

Keep in mind the type of FL you need, the industry experience, situational expertise, geography, and approximate fee amount you need from them and try to limit your reach-outs to those most likely to fit the bill.

Unfortunately, the information you need to filter your search for FLs who are an ideal fit for you isn't always on their websites or LinkedIn profiles. And even when it is, you have to dig through them one by one to find everything. And if the information is not there, you'll have to ask them using their contact forms or email information, or in introductory calls with them. Speak to as many people as you can and then narrow down your search to two to three finalists through that process.

Even though you'll learn a lot about what you are or are not looking for in all of these calls, they take a lot of time and band-width on your part—time and bandwidth you may not have.

I created www.FractionalLeadership.io (not .com) to make the process easier. I pre-vetted FLs in the areas of marketing, sales, operations, finance, and technology. You fill out a brief profile clarifying what you're looking for and your budget, and within two business days, my team emails you three referrals who fit what you're looking for and who have availability.

In the "Fractional Leader Referral Resources" section of Chapter 13, I also lay out several additional options that I think you will find very useful in finding FL candidates.

In-Person versus Remote Fit

If you know you'll only be comfortable with an in-person FL, ensure the people you're talking with can commit to that. If you are engaging with someone virtually, do you believe it's important to have an initial in-person meeting or day together with the team? If so, confirm before things go too far that the FL can do that.

Bandwidth Fit

Clarify your desired outcomes and ask yourself how much time they need to make those things happen. Then discuss that with your potential FLs. They've likely done what you're looking for before. You may find out that they can provide you with a reality check on how long things actually take. In my experience, business owners often underestimate the time and complexity involved in a project.

Now consider the bandwidth necessary to achieve the goals you so desperately want. Confirm whether your potential FL has that amount of time to commit.

If your potential FL can commit to the amount of time you need, ensure that their schedule is compatible with what you and your team need. If you need two days per week and your potential FL has two *full days* available per week but can't commit to time any other days of the week, does that work with you? Or do you need someone to spend half a day with you four days per week? You must ensure that compatibility before entering into an engagement.

Within Budget

If an FL is outside your budget for the time commitment you need to achieve results, it's best to find that out as soon as possible. Don't let the fact that it's sometimes difficult to speak about money cause you to waste your own time and theirs.

I was once talking with a potential client, a law firm. I had a spot opening up in a few weeks for a new client and we got into a deep conversation. I got to know what he was looking for and told him about what I'd done and could do for his business. It sounded like a great fit for both of us.

Then we began talking about specifics. I'd start off at one level of time commitment and then increase that in the second month. Finally, the amount of my retainer came up almost an hour into the conversation. It turned out that his maximum budget was about half of my monthly retainer! Oops. Wasted time for both of us.

After you've prequalified your potential FL with respect to the basics (industry experience, situational experience, desired outcomes, and time commitment necessary to achieve them), get retainers and billing rates on the table as soon as possible.

This will save you and your potential FLs time and make the process easier and faster.

Reference Checks

How can you have confidence that an FL can actually deliver results? How do you know they're not just talking a good game?

If you know someone who has used this person or you got the FL's name through a referral, that is ideal. If you don't have someone you know personally, ask the FL for three referrals from current or past FL clients. There is no foolproof method, but if you want some extra confidence in your final decision, references can be eye-opening.

Of course the FL will give you the names of people they believe will be positive references, but if you ask probing questions, you can still learn useful information. I've had some conversations with references that have strengthened my resolve to hire someone and others that have introduced new doubt about a candidate and spared me from retaining someone who may have been a bad fit.

I recommend calling references only as the very last step before signing on the dotted line with the one FL you want to hire. It's not fair to the FL or the busy business owners giving them a reference unless it is almost a done deal.

It's better if you use references who've worked with the FL in a fractional, rather than full-time, engagement. Why is it important that the references not be from one of the FL's previous full-time employers? Fractional Leadership requires a different set of skills than full-time employment. Simply because someone was a successful CFO does not mean that they will be a successful *Fractional* CFO.

Many executives who've only had full-time roles may not understand the differences between full-time and fractional work. One major difference between full-time work and fractional work is communication. For example, although it's also important for full-time people to communicate their accomplishments to their bosses, this is doubly important for FLs who are not there full-time and triply important for FLs working with you remotely.

Consider asking your potential FL's references some combination of the below probing questions:

- What did you engage the FL to do and what was your relationship with him or her in that engagement?

- How would you describe your overall satisfaction with the engagement?

- Please share a story or two when the FL provided excellent service.

- Please share a story or two when the FL disappointed you. How did they respond?

- Would you select this FL again knowing what you know today? Why or why not?

- Please share something else to backfill my understanding, something I should know but didn't ask about.

I particularly like the "Please share a story or two when the FL disappointed you. How did they respond?" question. Even great engagements with amazing FLs have had some bump in the road, hiccup, or challenge. That's not a reason, in and of itself, to disqualify someone.

This question draws out what happened and asks the more important question—"How did they respond?" You learn more about great people from how they handle missteps or misunderstandings than you do from purely glowing reports.

How to Set Up a Fractional Leadership Engagement Up for Success

Get a written agreement!

I once had one of those "Share a story when the FL disappointed you" moments before I'd even had my first day with one of my remote FL engagements. It may seem like an insignificant detail, but even though we had a written agreement, it did not address travel expense reimbursements.

I assumed it was obvious that because I was a contractor that I would invoice them for any travel expenses I incurred. And you know what they say happens when you assume...They thought that because I had left travel expenses out of the agreement that I would not seek reimbursement for those. Imagine their surprise when, before the first day I was going to spend physically with them when I sent them an invoice for travel expenses.

Fortunately, we were both straightforward and transparent communicators. The CEO told me he was taken aback by my invoice for something he thought was included in my retainer. I apologized for the ambiguity and explained why I'd assumed it was excluded. We agreed that I would send a revised agreement clarifying that point. Fortunately, that resolved the misunderstanding. In the end, we had a great first day and a great engagement. I can now offer him as a reference to future clients.

My story illustrates the point that you don't know what other reasonable people assume, so it's best to get your and the FL's expectations in writing because you never know when each side's expectations won't align.

The Written Agreement

Kwame Christian, Esq., Director of the American Negotiation Institute and author of *Finding Confidence in Conflict*, cautions against seeing conflict in the FL contract negotiation process as a bad thing. The worst approach you can take is to pull away from thorny questions or potential friction points by using a hope-based strategy of avoidance. Don't hide behind ambiguity with your fingers crossed that nothing will go wrong.

You can dive successfully and headlong into what Kwame calls constructive conflict by first triggering a mindset shift within yourself. Recognize that conflict isn't a bad thing. It's a positive opportunity to clear something up early on. He says, "All relationships, both business and personal, break down for the same reason. It isn't communication or trust, as many people believe. Those are symptoms of an underlying cause—frustrated expectations."

For example, Kwame suggests FLs say to business owners, "There are going to be times where I have to give you information that you don't want to hear and I need you to be okay with that. Let's talk about how that process takes place." By addressing the issue directly, everyone is on the same page when it does come to pass. He recommends:

> Start having these conversations from the very beginning. By setting that conversational pattern in the relationship, you keep both sides' expectations aligned and avoid the awkwardness and potentially relationship-killing fallout of having to broach a tough topic for the very first time six months into the engagement. And if talking over a thorny question at the contract negotiation stage reveals that the other side can't effectively engage in conflict, then it's probably not a good match to begin with. It's more important to discover that earlier rather than later.

Here are some things you should strongly consider clarifying in your agreement with your FL:

- Both parties' legal names

- Start date of the engagement

- Any specific accountabilities or deliverables, and by when they're due

- Any time commitment

- Any reporting obligations

- Compensation

- Frequency of payment

- Method of payment

- What happens if payments are not made on time

- How expenses are handled

- How vacation is handled, both theirs and yours

- Term and termination methods

- Notice method and requirements

- Applicable law and how any disputes are to be resolved

As discussed in the introductory paragraphs of this chapter, perhaps the most important of these is that you must talk through, and agree in writing, any specific accountabilities and deliverables your FL will provide and by when. Failure to clearly define outcomes and deliverables simply invites you as the business owner and your FL to fill in the gaps left by that lack of clarity based on preconceived notions—a recipe for disappointment and resentment.

Gary Braun, Partner at the FCSO firm Pivotal Advisors, says that he has seen engagements enter the danger zone when both sides neglected to clearly define the FL's accountabilities and how they would spend their time. In one case, the CEO pulled the FL into five different meetings starting on their first week, essentially using up the FL's entire day per week on meetings. He then wondered why the FCSO could not accomplish everything he expected.

Keep Your Fractional Leader in the Loop

Although some business owners are less conscious of it, each functional division of the organization is dependent on and interconnected with the others.

If, for example, you exclude an FCSO from decisions relating to operations, they won't have the information necessary to apprise the sales team of the training and workings of their product or service. Such decisions create or exacerbate hiccups in the handoff between sales and operations, leading to a rocky and disappointing customer experience.

FLs' wisdom and experience in multiple companies is a tremendous resource. Don't squander by isolating your FL only with people in the functional division for which they're responsible. Make the FL a full member of your leadership team who participates in its meetings and discussions.

Let us offer an example relating to an FCMO. Decisions relating to technology or finance affect marketing, sales, budget, and finance. It therefore adds value for you to involve your FCMO in those discussions. They can clue you in to the unforeseen consequences and ripple effects of various courses of action so you can ensure that you consider those factors in your leadership team's final decision making.

When I first started working with one client, their product and sales teams lacked a strong line of communication. When the product team introduced a new improvement or feature, no one told the sales team. There was virtually no product training. So none of the salespeople leveraged those new products, features, and improvements in their sales process. What a wasted opportunity!

It is critical to keep the communication lines open for another reason. Gary Braun describes what happens if a CEO and FL stop having their weekly one-on-one meetings because they're both so busy:

> They quickly get out of alignment. The CEO wonders what is happening; why have sales still not picked up, despite the fact that the FCSO has only been there for two months out of a nine-month sales cycle. They haven't heard from the FL. Meanwhile, the Fractional Leader is getting stuff done like crazy, but nobody knows about it. Or perhaps the FL is not even working on the things the CEO thinks are most important.

That is why it is so critical to keep the lines of communication open with your FL.

Next
You now understand:

- What Fractional Leadership is;

- How Fractional Leadership helps business owners break through the ceilings their businesses hit because it fills in the gaps of their and their leadership teams' experience building or running organizations of the scale they're at or want to achieve;

- How Fractional Leadership engagements generally work;

- Whether you're a candidate for utilizing an FL;

- How to determine what kind of FL you need;

- How to find the right FL for you; and

- How to set up your FL engagement for success before it even starts.

The next section of this book will dive into how the major types of Fractional Leadership (marketing, sales, operations, finance, and technology) work in more detail.

Part II

How the Major Types of Fractional Leadership Work to Break You through to the Next Level

WHAT HAPPENS WHEN YOU *DON'T* HAVE AN EXPERIENCED leader who's seen what you're going through before? What is it like when there is no one to give your team the tools and processes they need to avoid disaster and to succeed?

The Allies expected a major offensive by the Japanese around December 7, 1941, "a date which will live in infamy," as Roosevelt called it. They did not, however, expect it at Pearl Harbor, Hawaii just before 8:00 a.m. They thought the attack would come somewhere in the South Pacific or in the Philippines.

On that fateful morning, Lieutenant Kermit Tyler, an army fighter pilot, was assigned to supervise the aircraft tracking center at Fort Shafter, near the Pearl Harbor naval base. It was his first day on the job. The radar technology was new, and the army hadn't established any protocols for what to do if the radar operators saw anything. They gave Lt. Tyler no training or any process for distinguishing between what was normal and what should raise the alarm.

If you're a business owner or leader, you likely relate to the army's approach there—trying out something new with no procedures, processes, or training.

At about 7:00 a.m., Lt. Tyler received a phone call from a nearby radar station. Two army privates reported picking up a large group of approaching planes. He thought that these were probably B-17s the Allies were expecting to arrive that day from the east (not from the west, like this cluster).

Tyler also failed to take the report seriously because it was the radar operator's first day on the job too. His response was, as he told *The San Diego Union-Tribune* in an interview in 2000, "I figured they were pretty green and had not had any opportunity to view a flight of B-17s coming in. Common sense said, Well, these are the B-17s. So I told them, 'Don't worry about it.'"

It turned out that what the radio operators saw was the first wave of Japanese bombers and fighters that ultimately destroyed virtually all the ships at Battleship Row, killed over 2,400 people, and plunged the United States into World War II. The two green radar operators had first detected these planes an hour before the Pearl Harbor bombing.

That same morning, just before dawn, the USS *Ward* sank a Japanese navy "midget submarine" using depth charges just as it was trying to enter Pearl Harbor. These submarines were so-named because they were small and were transported by and launched from larger submarines.

If people had been paying attention, the discovery of the small sub about 4,000 miles from Japan would have aroused suspicions. Perhaps it should have alerted them that the prevailing notion that the Japanese would attack somewhere in the South Pacific or the Philippines was mistaken. How could the submarine have gotten so far from Japan unless it was part of a larger fleet?

Neither the discovery of the sub nor the fleet of planes spotted by the novice radar operators was enough to warn US forces of the impending attack on Pearl Harbor.

When your business is at a scale you've never experienced before, you don't know what to look for. You don't know what's normal and what's abnormal. So what do you do? Confirmation bias takes over. You approach everything the way that worked for you when you were in all-hands-on-deck startup mode. But you discover that what got you here isn't getting you where you want to go next. You don't know how to handle the wrenches the world throws into your gears or the obstacles blocking your path.

That's why it's so critical to involve leaders who have the specific knowledge and experience you need to get your business from where it is to where you want it to go. You need someone who's already seen what you're going through and can guide you on what to do. Then the unexpected challenges and curveballs life throws at you will no longer take you by surprise or sink your battleship.

The Five Categories of Fractional Leadership
In the next several chapters, I will outline some high-level considerations and offer some insight into how the five major

types of Fractional Leadership work: marketing, sales, operations, finance, and technology.

The information in this chapter is a consolidation of my personal experience as an FL, retaining other FLs in businesses I managed or manage, interviews with FLs on my podcast, *Win Win—An Entrepreneurial Community*, and my network and relationships with other FLs.

My experience in operations and of being an FI in companies running on EOS certainly contribute to the chapters on operations. I am not, however, a subject matter expert in marketing, sales, finance, or technology. These sections are therefore written in reliance on business owners and FLs in those fields—from a 30,000 foot perspective.

In each chapter, I start by painting a picture of what things look like in your business *before* engaging with an experienced FL. What are the pain points? What are the most common challenges?

I follow that with a description of the most common stages of the relevant Fractional Leadership engagements and how they work.

At the end of each chapter, I point out several questions you should ask yourself or the FL to ensure that you pick the right one.

I address each major type of Fractional Leadership in the order their domains of expertise arise in the sales and fulfillment cycle: marketing, sales, operations, finance, and technology.

So without further ado, we will start with marketing.

6.

Marketing

How to Stop Wasting Money on "Random Acts of Marketing" with a Fractional Chief Marketing Officer (FCMO)

BEFORE EOS WORLDWIDE GREW BIG ENOUGH TO HIRE a full-time CMO, they retained Marisa Smith, owner and founder of The Whole Brain Group, as its FCMO for four years. Although EOS founder Gino Wickman transitioned out of the organization as its full-time Visionary around the time Marisa joined in 2014, he told me:

> Marisa Smith was a rock star. She took us to a whole other level as a fractional marketing leader. It worked phenomenally. It was a classic example of us not being able to afford the person we needed full-time so we paid for a fraction of that until we grew into it and could afford 100 percent of the right person's time.

When Marisa joined EOS Worldwide, she initially committed to spending about ten hours per week with the organization and serving on its leadership team. She continued in that role on a fractional basis, continually building its marketing infrastructure until the organization was ready to transition to a full-time CMO. Like other great FLs, Marisa helped them find the right full-time marketing leader to replace her.[26]

During her tenure, her work, intertwined with everyone else's on EOS Worldwide's leadership team, grew the organization by 400 percent. Like any other FCMO engagement, Marisa helped put into place a lead generation process and brand standards, exponentially grew their email list and website traffic, developed content marketing, and tackled many other endeavors.

What It Looks Like without an FCMO

So let's paint a picture of what things look and feel like *before* your firm engages an FCMO.

Most of your marketing efforts are scattershot without a clearly defined story and message geared toward a clearly defined target market that runs through every single thing you do.

You're frustrated with the declining results you're seeing from your sales and marketing and know you need to step up your game or things will fall apart.

You're also frustrated with and know marketing agencies are no longer the answer for your particular problem because they require so much of your or your team's time to direct and supervise, or perhaps they just don't *get* what you need.

---

26 She loved EOS so much that during her time there, she decided to become a Professional EOS Implementer for other organizations. So when she left EOS Worldwide as its FCMO, she pursued that dream and is now a Certified EOS Implementer based in Ann Arbor, Michigan.

Your company has a gross revenue of $5–$50 million. Most of your growth was based on your strength in sales.

You've probably never had a marketing leader who has "been there and done that" as a partner with a sales organization and cannot afford one full-time.

You have or can get more tactical, in-the-trenches marketing help internally or through vendors, but you recognize that you may be throwing away money on this without an FCMO to take over strategic leadership of these resources.

Three Main Situations

There are three types of business owners who start searching for an FCMO.

In one, the CEO, founder, or Head of Sales drives marketing, but because they have no extensive experience or bandwidth to drive marketing strategically, it sits on the back burner, is reactive, and turns into "random acts of marketing."

A second scenario is where you, as the business owner, have outsourced marketing to one or more external partners. The problem arises when, because you've outsourced your brand, the consultant never "gets it" the way an in-house leader with close collaboration with your leadership team and sales organization would.

In the third common situation, you, as the business owner, have hired what you thought would be a "unicorn," a one-person marketing wizard, at a low price point, with two to five years' marketing experience who can do *everything* (events, blog posts, social media, PPC, strategy, writing all content, collateral design, and running the website).

The "unicorn" marketing person could be great as part of a team under the leadership of an experienced CMO or FCMO. But no one person can do all aspects of marketing, no matter how young or digitally savvy. Often, the business owner blames the marketer as not being good enough. But the reality is that almost no one with that level of experience can take ownership over what a growing business needs from marketing at their size and scale. You and the marketer were set up for disappointment and failure from the beginning.

How an FCMO Makes You Money

How does an FCMO make you money and not simply end up as a cost center? Typically, you hire an FCMO because you're throwing away money. You've hit the tipping point where sales have plateaued and you're not getting enough leads (or at least not enough qualified ones).

You keep turning up the lever that used to work swimmingly (ad spend), but sales conversions are getting worse and you're selling less because sales spends all of its time qualifying leads.

An in-house FCMO has seen and done this before. They've experienced that problem and will make both your marketing and sales more effective by ensuring that fewer of the wrong leads come in and more of the right ones start responding to your ads and organic marketing. That way, your salespeople can spend more time actually selling instead of qualifying leads.

How Typical FCMO Engagements Work

Jennifer Zick of Authentic Brand (a Fractional CMO firm) cautions against a tactics-driven approach to marketing.[27] Many growing businesses wrongly assume that marketing campaigns, programs, channels, or technologies will unlock their growth potential.

Although tools and tactics are necessary, they must first be grounded in a strong vision, clear go-to-market focus, unique value proposition, and authentic story. As one of Zick's past colleagues used to say, "If you build a marketing stack on a weak story, all that does is make your story suck faster to more people."

The best marketing begins with—and is grounded in—brand clarity. Skipping this essential ingredient will only result in what Authentic Brand calls random acts of marketing, which ultimately leads to frustration over wasted resources, lost time, and lack of predictable growth.

Target Market and Message

The most important and one of the earliest things FCMOs typically focus on is creating or developing your brand's target market and message. That is your essential story to your potential customers or clients. It resonates with them because it shows you understand what's actually bothering them and then shows how you fill the gap or solve their needs.

---

27 "How to Have a Marketing Strategy rather than 'Random Acts of Marketing: Interview with Jennifer Zick," *Win Win—An Entrepreneurial Community* podcast, episode 13, August 19, 2019, https://podcasts.apple.com/us/podcast/013-how-to-have-marketing-strategy-rather-than-random/id1465488607?i=1000447240281.

Aren't we all customers to someone? As a human being, when I have an issue or search on the internet for something I need, when I see ads or read websites for companies who try to be all things to all people, I innately recognize that this means they're not an expert in what I need.

Even though all of us are customers or clients, we somehow forget what it's like to be a consumer when it comes to our own businesses. We extol our product's or service's virtues. We, not our client or customer, are the hero of our story. We try to be the solution to all problems because we're afraid of losing any potential business. That does not resonate with most people.

An FCMO gets to know you but more importantly, gets to know your customers or clients. He or she typically begins by clarifying your brand message and story—a story in which your customers or clients are the protagonists of their own stories.

Metrics

The only metric that counts is revenue. How do you know what's throwing money away and what gets you more revenue?

Once your target market and brand message or story are clear, your FCMO will incorporate that into your marketing. But if you're not clear on what activities drive your revenue, you can't judge the success or failure of any particular message, type of media, or strategy.

FCMOs therefore typically determine the activities or metrics that drive your revenue. Those include things like number of website leads, number of content videos or articles produced, number of phone leads, number of emails captured, and the like. Once these metrics are clear, your FCMO will determine how to capture them, ensure you're measuring them regularly, and that you have or obtain the tools necessary to judge the success or failure of your marketing efforts.

Driving Execution

Finally, your FCMO is the captain of your marketing ship. He or she directs your internal marketing team or external vendors to execute on the plan and continually iterate it.

Your FCMO will drive the copywriting, creatives, events, or whatever the marketing plan they created involves. They will drive action on those activities or media that speak to your specific target market with a message that resonates with them.

They will often use A/B testing to determine which messages or images resonate best and will hold themselves and your marketing team (whether internal or external) accountable to achieving results through those efforts.

They will continually review and evolve marketing systems, data, media channels, and content. They will ensure that your content creation is consistent and ongoing because that is what achieves results and ultimately makes you the go-to source for customers who need what you do.

People develop trust and relationships with people, not brands, at least in the entrepreneurial space. Your FCMO may therefore help you leverage your and your people's connections, network, and relationships to share your content and make more impact on your potential customers.

They will infer the average value of each client acquisition based on length and revenue from past engagements ("deal value"). They will also determine a "cost per acquisition" for each "deal" and discover what your current "conversion rate" is so you can judge any marketing idea's potential return on investment.

If you don't have some of this data, the FCMO will lead the effort to put that together. Without data-based decision making, you cannot make intelligent decisions about what to do and what not to do, or about what is or isn't working. You'd be just operating on gut and instinct. Your FCMO will drive the creation and analysis of that data over time.

As necessary and appropriate, they will create a hiring plan and onboard and train new marketing team members or select new vendors to augment your capabilities. They will collaborate with other members of the leadership team in whatever they do to ensure that their efforts are in concert with the other major functions of your business.

Your FCMO will very often stay as part of your business for one to two years. Engagements sometimes last longer, but very often if they've done their job, you've scaled to the point where you may need or want a full-time CMO. They will facilitate the transition to your full-time CMO. That is not a disappointment to them. It's the goal of what they consider to be a successful engagement not just for you but for themselves too.

Do You Need a Marketing Agency, Consultant, or FCMO?

How do you know whether you should engage with a marketing agency or consultant rather than with an FCMO?

The short answer is that marketing consultants are generally right for short-term, discrete projects like setting up your target market, brand messaging, creatives, a new website, or a rebrand. If you have the bandwidth and internal leadership to supervise the consultant and then carry out all the follow-through that naturally comes after their project, then this may be a good option for you.

If, however, you lack that internal bandwidth, you may be throwing away a lot of money by hiring a consultant because you'll lack the focused attention to oversee the engagement while it's going on, as well as for the follow-up execution afterward. You won't get the full advantage of what you retained them to do.

Marketing agencies can oversee ongoing pay-per-click, print, email, blog, content marketing, videos, or other kinds of marketing campaigns on an ongoing basis. But who's overseeing them? Who's ensuring that their efforts are part of a cohesive strategy? Do you or does someone on your team know what to look for so that the money you're spending with them isn't going to waste? Are they continually iterating and improving? Are the messages they're putting into the world on your behalf consistent with what your salespeople are saying and communicating? Do they reflect a message that demonstrably *gets* your clients or customers the way you do?

If you or someone on your team has the experience and bandwidth to oversee a marketing consultant or agency's work and can continually ensure its effectiveness and consistency with your business and its clients, then that's great! Those are likely the best resources for you, especially in your earlier stages of growth.

But if you don't have the bandwidth to oversee their efforts in a robust way, an FCMO is a great and cost-effective resource. He or she can give you a fast, low-risk way to bring that experience, expertise, and bandwidth in-house to ensure you're getting the biggest bang for your precious marketing buck.

Time Commitment and Cost

I have seen FCMOs who work with only two clients at a time, about twenty hours per week each, and others who are with their clients about one day per week. Each FCMO and each business is different, so there is no one right way. Once you discuss your needs with potential FCMOs, you will start to realize the scale of engagement that is right for you.

Engagements range from $6,000 per month for about a day per week to $18,000 per month for half time. This varies greatly and depends on the local market you're in and/or they're in. It also depends on the FCMO's level of experience.

Questions to Ask Potential FCMOs

Ask potential FCMOs to tell you about the marketing teams (including both external vendors and internal teams) they've built or led. You want to find someone who hasn't just been a solo consultant where they did all the heavy lifting themselves. Even if they did a great job as a solo practitioner, this does not mean they can do it at the CMO level for you if they haven't successfully done that before.

Find out whether your potential FCMO has been a CMO fractionally before and inquire about that experience. As explained in Chapter 5, "How to Find the Right Fractional

Leader for Maximum Impact," fractional C-level leadership requires different skills than full-time leadership. Even those FCMOs who have successfully been full-time C-level executives before may not succeed in a fractional engagement.

If they seem primarily and initially very tactics focused, this may be a bit of a red flag. The vast majority of the great CMOs I've met and heard from almost always emphasize target market, story, and message before they get into specific tactics. If they start with tactics, it may indicate that they don't understand strategic marketing leadership.

Probe whether the FCMO is on the same page with you regarding the purpose of marketing in your business. Is it purely and only a lead generation tool—performance marketing? Or are you looking for building brand and reputation for the longer term—brand marketing? This type of distinction will make a huge difference in their focus.

If you're out of sync on what kind of outcomes you're looking for, then the whole experience will be very frustrating for both of you. Clearly explain what's important to you without any embarrassment and ask them to explain their point of view or plan on that.

Next

If your marketing is in good (or good enough) shape, learn in the next chapter how to ensure your sales team capitalizes on the demand created by your marketing by engaging a Fractional Chief Sales Officer.

7.

Sales

Create a Whole Team of "A Players" with a
Fractional Chief Sales Officer (FCSO)

ALICE[28] FOUNDED CENTURION SECURITY AND BUILT IT
into an $8 million national distributor of security hardware
such as cameras, door access, building control systems using
AI, and motion-activated lights. She was frustrated because no
matter what she tried, the company could not grow beyond
that $8 million level. They were simply hitting a wall and didn't
know why. She wanted to grow Centurion into a $13 million
venture over the next two years but didn't know how to do it.

Alice wanted to hire an experienced Head of Sales but
simply could not afford someone like that with her current
revenues and profit margin. She heard about Fractional
Leadership and wanted to give it a try. An FCSO doesn't require the same commitment as a new full-time, leadership-level
hire, so she figured it would be a good way to ease her way
into hiring someone full-time later on.

A colleague of Alice's in a peer advisory group recommended

---

28 All names have been changed.

Kendley Davenport, President of Outsourced Sales Pros, as an FCSO. She engaged him to help her break through the sales ceiling.

First, because Kendley had built and managed many sales organizations over the years, he noticed that Centurion's sales process was completely reactive. When prospective or existing customers called their salespeople, the sales team sold them whatever they ordered. Sounds simple enough. But they were neglecting their customers' true needs and leaving money on the table.

Kendley trained the salespeople to find out why their customers were asking for whichever product they called about. What was motivating them? What problems were they trying to solve? What outcomes did they need to achieve?

Here is one example. Most of Centurion's clients were not the end users. They were system integrators (technology or security system installers). One client in Virginia called their salesperson at Centurion about sensors to detect when transformers blew out. Because of the new sales training, the salesperson asked why the integrator's client needed sensors to detect blown-out transformers. What exactly was their situation?

It turns out that the utility company who hired the system integrator (Centurion's client) had to avoid power grid downtime because Virginia happens to be the largest concentration of data centers in the world. Ninety percent of the world's internet is routed, one way or another, through those data centers. Maintaining power there is critical. The utility had to replace burned-out transformers ASAP. The reliability of the entire internet literally depended on it.

When the salesperson learned about the problem his client was solving for the utility company, he volunteered a new solution to make the system integrator the hero, increase his *and* Centurion's sales, and save the utility company, the end user, tons of money.

Instead of detecting when a transformer had *already* blown, the Centurion salesperson told his client about temperature sensors they offered that were capable of detecting changes in equipment temperature from up to 500 feet away. These systems would allow the utility company to replace a transformer *before* it blew out. At that point, it costs only around $4,000 to replace the transformer, rather than the $200,000 it cost the utility to replace the transformer after it had already blown.

By finding out about the client's underlying goals, Centurion sold these temperature detection systems for around $35,000 per site at dozens of sites per year over several years. Furthermore, each of these systems involve security system subscriptions that create recurring revenue for both Centurion and its system integrator client. Best of all, they are now both heroes because the utility company now saves $196,000 on every single transformer it is able to replace before it blows out. A win-win-win.

These are the kind of opportunities you find and problems you solve by engaging the help of someone who's done this before, knows what to look for, and understands how to drive you and your team toward the achievement of your dreams and goals.

What's Happening That's Making You Think of Hiring an FCSO?

In my conversion with Teresa Renaud, an FCSO affiliated with SalesQB, she explains three main scenarios that trigger the need for an FCSO.[29]

In the first, you're personally "half-managing" the sales team. You don't have a Head of Sales you can trust or rely on, or because you're the best at sales, so you're running the team. I say "half-managing" because you have an entire business to run, not just sales, so your full attention simply isn't on it. You don't have the bandwidth to develop a proven sales process, figure out how to collect and use data to hold the team accountable for actual sales results, and you don't have the time to teach, manage, and coach the sales team to excellence the way they need. You're frustrated with the results.

The second scenario is one where you hired a sales leader or manager at a lower price point because you can't afford more or don't see sales management as hard. You underestimated the skills and experience you need your sales leader to have. Now you have an underperforming sales manager who's frustrating you and the team. All the salespeople still go to you almost all of the time anyway, they're frustrated, and the sales manager is one more person you have to manage. He isn't saving you any time.

In the third scenario, you decided to take your best salesperson and make him or her the sales manager or team leader. They

---

29 "How to Free Up from Half-Managing an Underperforming Sales Team: Interview with Teresa Renaud," *Win Win—An Entrepreneurial Community* podcast, episode 54, July 21, 2020, https://podcasts.apple.com/us/podcast/054-how-to-free-up-from-half-managing-underperforming/id1465488607?i=1000485649903.

either take a passive role, simply answering other salespeople's questions, leaving them with essentially no manager at all. Or they try to live up to that role but aren't good at managing people, creating systems and processes, collecting data, or using that data to hold the team accountable. You've now lost your best salesperson, so sales are down, and you still don't have an effective sales leader for everyone else. It's the worst of both worlds.

The common denominator in all of these scenarios is a recognition that being a good salesperson is a completely different skillset from leadership, management of people, and creation of accountability.

To get past this blockage, you want someone who's built and led sales teams successfully before. Presumably you're reading this book because you can't yet afford someone with that level of experience full-time.

How Does an FCSO Engagement Work?

Here are a few of the main elements an FCSO will typically tackle for you. Depending on the situation in your business, your FCSO will tackle the various elements of a powerful sales team in different orders.

They will lock down your lead generation process and head up your marketing efforts. The way this will work depends on whether you have someone in your marketing seat or whether you'll need your FCSO to fulfill that role as well.

They will ensure that whatever you're doing for lead generation gets you leads who are in your target market and that you have the correct information for them. Your salespeople shouldn't have to waste unnecessary time qualifying the leads they get; they should spend their time selling.

As part of locking down the lead generation process, the FCSO may create a scoring system to ensure that there is accountability for the quality, as well as the quantity, of leads. This sometimes involves an additional step for salespeople in ranking the quality of leads, or at least a sampling of them. The team may complain. But in the long term, accountable quality lead generation will save them far more time than it would take to properly score their leads.

Next is the sales process itself. Right now, each salesperson may have their own sales method and each has different messages. Presumably, your best salespeople have discovered the best and most effective ways to reach people and have identified the most resonant messages. Your FCSO will draw on your and your sales team's experience to clarify and document the right and best way to do sales in your unique organization with your unique customer or client base.

He or she will create metrics around the actions you know drive results in sales (e.g., the number of emails, calls, demos, or proposals sent per week). They will establish minimums around those metrics and set up a meeting pulse to create accountability around the actual frequency of those activities.

They will determine how best to use technology like a CRM to manage these metrics and create actionable data. Using this data, you'll find out how many of each type of action you need to get the results you want.

The data they'll help you use will also make you better at predicting how many salespeople you need and seeing when people need extra help.

The FCSO will take ownership over building up your sales team when appropriate by driving recruiting, interviewing, hiring, and training to build a team of "A players."

They will help you determine the right compensation plan for salespeople to align their personal goals with your organization's goals.

The FCSO will manage, train, and coach your sales team on an ongoing basis through weekly team meetings, holding people accountable to the new metrics, and giving salespeople the support they need when they're underperforming so they can be successful.

Very often, they will shadow calls or meetings with clients, either over the phone, by joining meetings, or by listening to recordings after the fact. They will use these experiences not only as a tool for sales training but also as an intelligence-gathering tool to continually improve and iterate the sales process.

Your FCSO will create corrective action plans with underperforming salespeople and make the difficult decision to let someone go when it becomes apparent that they aren't going to be able to level up.

Managing the Sales Team When the FCSO Isn't Around

Chris White and Benj Miller asked me on the *System & Soul* podcast how an FCSO can manage a sales team when they aren't there most of the time.[30] As I wrote in Chapter 3, "What Fractional Leadership Engagements Look Like So You Know Exactly What to Expect," I explained how FCSOs don't work the way business owners still in startup mode do. It's not about helicopter management.

---

30 Chris White and Benj Miller, "Fractional Leadership Fit with Benjamin Wolf," *System & Soul* podcast, episode 67, November 2020, https://open.spotify.com/episode/2CU2FF50 vYn4FIbW58VZYc?si=qvvtRTa7Ta-6ZpTZvi3Lrg.

The FCSO develops a documented sales process and then establishes specific metrics that drive sales based on that process. They then hold the team accountable to achieving those results at a weekly sales meeting.

There's no hiding from numbers. If people don't use your CRM to track their calls or emails, or if they don't do those calls or emails, it doesn't matter whether the FCSO was there to make sure they did it throughout the week. If they don't do what they need to, that will be apparent.

If you have your FCSO's back, he or she can coach, train, and mentor the sales team into excellence using the tools you know will work and get you more sales. And for those who can't despite the support and coaching they're getting, your FCSO will help you make the tough decisions to ensure everyone on your sales team gets, wants, and has the capacity to do their jobs well.

Organizational FCSOs, Individual CSOs, and Sales Management Licensees

In Chapter 3, I discussed several different models of Fractional Leadership, but some of those have a special application when it comes to the FCSO market.

Some FCSOs operate as a group under one umbrella—which I call organizational Fractional Leaders (OFLs). You engage with an FCSO firm and they work with you to find you an experienced FCSO from their firm to serve on your leadership team. The advantage of this model is that your FCSO has a proven process used by the OFL and is part of a group he or she can look to, all as part of the engagement, for ideas or additional resources in solving your unique challenges. Another advantage of the OFL model is the firm's ability to switch FCSOs for you if something does not work out with one person.

Other business owners engage with solo practitioners—that is, individual, "single shingle" FCSOs. They like the independence and greater simplicity of working with a single individual. If that person has the right experience, then this often works very well.

Some independent FCSOs are licensees of an established sales management system. The two main licensing organizations are SalesQB, founded by Jim Muehlhausen, and Sales Xceleration, founded by Mark Thacker.

The advantage of this model is that you know the person you're retaining uses a tried-and-true system for sales management and that they come with tools custom-designed for growing small and midsize businesses' sales.

There are great FCSOs using all the above models, so you really need to ask yourself which resonates more with you. Speak with FCSOs or clients who have used the various models to determine which would be best for you.

Time Commitment and Cost

FCSOs have a wide variety of time commitment options. Some spend two half days per month, a half day per week, or one day per week with their clients. Others commit even more time.

As with other types of Fractional Leadership, FCSOs have a wide range of prices. Some charge by the hour, but most use a monthly retainer. Hourly rates can range from $100–$250 per hour, and I have seen monthly retainers starting at $1,500 per month for two half days per month or $2,500/month for a half day each week, to \$5,000–\$15,000 per month for one day per week.

The amount and time commitment necessary depend, as always, on the experience level of the FCSO and the local market both for yourself and the FCSO.

Questions to Ask before You Engage an FCSO

Like any other kind of FL, you want to define the deliverables you expect from your FCSO before the engagement starts. Discuss your current sales and what you expect him or her to achieve and in what time frame. This is a critical conversation because if he or she believes those expectations are unrealistic or that they are not the right person to achieve your goals, you want to clarify that up front.

Discuss the level of authority you can and are willing to grant the FCSO. Like other types of FLs, they will work collaboratively with you on major decisions. But do they have the right to, if necessary and after exhausting other reasonable options, terminate people's employment? Do they have the right to shop and make buying decisions on tools they believe the team needs? Can they incur travel or other kinds of expenses?

The main thing is to ensure that the two of you are 100 percent on the same page to avoid misunderstanding, frustration, or disappointment later on.

Next

If your marketing or sales are not your biggest pain point right now but you're having pervasive issues with your people, business structure, or processes, your main pain point may be your operations. The next two chapters explain how to use Fractional Chief Operating Officers or, for companies using the Entrepreneurial Operating System management framework, Fractional Integrators.

8.

Operations

How a Fractional Chief Operating Officer (FCOO) Makes You More Scalable with the Right Structure and Processes

JOHN NEMO, FOUNDER AND CEO OF THE NEMO MEDIA Group, lives in Saint Paul, Minnesota. He created his agency ten years ago to provide lead generation and customized content marketing services for executive and business coaches and other small business owners.

By the time he found Leah Leaves, he was drowning in busywork. Based in Colorado, Leah provides FCOO services through her company, Alderaan Business Solutions. At that time, John had six team members but was still leading all of the firm's business functions by himself. He was constantly consumed with sales, project and client management, hiring and recruiting, and the actual marketing strategy and implementation work for his firm's clients.

John was still making sales, but the quality of work he was able to provide was diminishing. Desperate to get his service delivery under control, he retained Leah because she specializes in being the "right-hand woman" for digital marketing agency founders like himself.

During her first two months with Nemo, Leah set them up with processes and procedures to stop John from becoming the bottleneck and standardize the team's delivery while eliminating time-wasting inefficiencies. The last thing John, or any business owner, wants is to sacrifice the personal feeling clients get working with a small company or the morale and close-knit culture the small team enjoyed. Leah scaled Nemo's processes in a way that would ensure that clients and employees had a great experience.

She developed regular performance incentives and professional development opportunities so that everyone on the team felt like they were constantly competing with their own past accomplishments, achieving greater results, feeling satisfied and successful, and like they were growing as professionals.

Within eight months, Nemo Media Group grew from six to eighteen people and doubled their revenue while maintaining a strong profit margin despite the increased head count.

Although each FCOO engagement looks different depending on the industry, founder's personal style and values, and the size of the organization, one thing they usually have in common is improved team health, standardized better processes, tangible traction toward goals, and less stress. It also means business owners finally regain the feeling of satisfaction and enjoyment from the businesses they founded.

What It's Like Now

Ken Trupke, founder of FCOO firm Verant Partners, says:

> Typically for a fractional role, the owner is the founder and he or she started it. It's now gotten to a point that their span of control is too broad. The business is really limited by their ability to touch everything. They had an idea and took it, ran with it, and really enjoyed the customer interaction, but not so much the day-to-day operations. They're just unfulfilled. The owner-founder started the business with this vision of freedom and lifestyle and interacting with customers and now she's bogged down with people issues and it's just gotten bigger than what they want to deal with on a day-to-day basis.[31]

You're suffering from broad-based or generalized pain. You're frustrated with poor cash flow, stagnant business growth, increasing overhead, or low or dipping conversion rates. Perhaps your operations can't keep pace with your sales or they are slow or mistake-ridden. You might be suffering from high turnover or low morale. You've tried a number of solutions, but nothing has worked and you're simply not sure what to do about it.

You've grown big enough so that you can no longer afford to continue without operations leadership, but you're not yet big enough to afford a COO with the kind of experience you desperately need on a full-time basis.

In some instances, people are ready to hire (or replace) a

---

31 "Your Issue Is People, Not Process: Interview with Fractional COO Ken Trupke," *Win Win—An Entrepreneurial Community* podcast, episode 69, November 10, 2020, https:// podcasts.apple.com/us/podcast/069-your-issue-is-people-not-process-interview-fractional/ id1465488607?i=1000497991964.

COO full-time but know that the selection of the right person is so critical that they don't want to rush it and are willing to spend the six to eighteen months it might take to find the right person. They engage with an FCOO on an interim basis because they cannot afford to leave that seat unfilled and lose precious momentum during the search process.

Doer Leaders and Manager Leaders

In terms of size and scale, I've seen two major types of businesses engaging the help of an FCOO. I'll call them small businesses (SBs) and midsized business (MSBs).

If you're an SB, you're probably in the five-to-twenty-person size range. You have one person, or maybe no one besides yourself, the business owner, on your leadership team. You need help with organizational structure, processes, and better data, but you also need someone to simply get higher-level stuff done. I call the kind of FCOO you need a Doer Leader. The story of the FCOO engaged by Rachel Beider, founder and CEO of Press Modern Massage, from Chapter 4, "How to Figure Out Whether You're a Candidate for Fractional Leadership," is a great example of the kind of Doer Leader many SBs need.

If you're an MSB, you're probably in the 20–250 person size range and have a leadership team of two or more people. Your main need for an FCOO is the leadership of someone who's already built a business as big or bigger than yours. You need their leadership and experience to put in place the structure, data, management systems, and processes you need to get healthy, successful, scalable, and strong. You need an FCOO to hold your and your leadership teams' hands and for their leadership, management, and ability to create accountability and discipline. You don't need someone to *personally* get stuff done. I call this kind of person a Manager Leader.

There are both Doer Leader and Manager Leader FCOOs custom-made for both SBs and MSBs.

Doer Leaders

FCOOs of this type typically come at a lower price point relative to Manager Leaders. Business owners often engage them for one day per week or more. Because, in addition to their leadership role, they're also doing more tactical operations leadership or getting multiple cross-functional projects done so you don't have to, they may work two or two and a half days per week.

Manager Leaders

This brand of FCOO typically has experience with larger organizations and engages with their clients at a higher level to determine the right structure for an organization, define its goals, establish the right metrics to ensure it achieves those goals, and then drive implementation of those goals at the leadership team level of the organization.

These FCOOs typically, though not always, work for about one day per week or less. They frequently come at a higher price point relative to Manager Leader FCOOs for the same time commitment because of the more strategic nature of their leadership and their experience running larger organizations.

How FCOO Engagements Typically Work

Ken Trupke recently began two client engagements, both of which were manufacturers. The first company was founded by a seventy-year-old father. The son was soon going to take over the company. They used the same equipment and people that they had since the 1990s for their operations and had not innovated at all. Unfortunately for them, the internet and Chinese manufacturing had happened in the meantime and the business was in steady decline.

The other company was doing well but faced a sudden crisis when they lost four large clients within about four weeks, reducing their revenue from $12 million to $8 million. They needed to determine whether they should close down or cut whatever they could and invest in rebuilding the company.

In both instances, Ken was working with community businesses with a lot of pride in the way they'd supported their neighbors and created jobs. Neither could afford a full-time COO to come in and save the company, so they asked Ken to help fractionally. He helped both companies cut where they could and prioritize where and how to invest to improve their people, equipment, and processes to right their ships.

Ken worked over several quarters to rehabilitate the businesses and prepare them for long-term, full-time management. When he succeeded in building the internal infrastructure they needed to operate successfully, he moved on.

What Will Your FCOO Engagement Look Like?

Begin with the end in mind. This is the typical mantra of FCOOs. At the beginning of an engagement, they will work with you to learn about your business and determine where you are now and where you want to go.

Once you've determined that, they will work with you to map out a plan for how to get you from point A to point Z. Depending on the critical issues weighing you down or causing you the most pain, they may tackle people issues, data issues, or process issues first.

If people issues loom largest in your organization, they may take a blank-slate approach and revisit your entire organizational structure and determine the right roles and structure for your business. They'll then clearly define what each role should be responsible for. Once that is clear, they will help drive implementation of that new structure. Some people's positions may need to change. Other people may no longer have a place in the organization.

Your FCOO will lead implementation of this better structure firmly and inexorably but as gently as possible, taking people's feelings into account. Change is hard and people usually resist it. Giving people context, transparency, and the reason for changes makes it easier. But it will not be easy.

If process issues are predominant, your FCOO will help you map out the current processes causing you the most issues and come up with a solution. This may involve simply agreeing on a right and best way to do things, documenting that, training people on it, and then establishing metrics and/or management systems to ensure that people carry out the new processes. Depending on your industry, this may involve purchasing equipment or implementing or modifying a CRM or ERP to manage your processes and workflows differently.

In any scenario, your FCOO will likely determine the metrics or Key Performance Indicators (KPIs) which give you an accurate pulse on how you're doing and allow you to look around the corner to see issues before they get too far gone.

This means, for example, looking at sales activities like calls made, proposals sent, or qualified leads generated, rather than just sales closed. The former give you a glimpse of what your sales next month will be (so you can still do something about it), while the latter simply tells you the impact of the actions you took last month.

If successful, your FCOO will help you grow and scale in a way you could never do on your own. They will ultimately help you interview full-time COO candidates, collaborate with you in the hiring process, and then transition the new COO in. Alternatively, using your new structure and processes, you may be able to transition the head of operations role to someone internally. The FCOO can help you train and mentor that person to level them up into the role.

Time Commitment and Cost

As with other kinds of FLs, time commitment and cost vary greatly. These differences correspond to the differences between Doer Leader and Manager Leader FCOOs.

Doer Leader FCOOs typically work with their clients for between one and two and a half days per week. Some charge an hourly rate, at a rate of $100–$150 per hour. And others use a monthly retainer of $4,000–$6,000 per month for each day of the week they spend with their clients. So if a particular FCOO charges $5,000 per month per day of the week, that would be $10,000 per month for two days and $12,500 for two and a half days per week.

Manager Leader FCOOs sometimes charge per hour but usually work on a monthly retainer. Monthly amounts range from $6,000 to $13,000 per day-of-the-week spent with clients.

What to Ask before Engaging with an FCOO

As with any type of FL, clearly communicate your desired outcomes and deliverables. This enables you to perform a gut check on what you want to see and ensure that you are on the same page with your potential FCOO.

Make sure the FCOOs you're speaking with have the relevant industry experience if that is important. Very often, specific industry experience is not relevant. Many FCOOs have worked in a variety of industries and their main value proposition is their management, organization, and process skills. Any expertise with respect to specific industries is frequently, though not always, less relevant.

But you know your business best. If you believe the learning curve is just too great in your business and would take too long, then you must ensure, in advance, that the FCOO you're speaking with has the industry experience you need.

You may need your FCOO's help on a specific kind of activity or transaction, whether that's an M&A transaction, a due diligence process, a new product rollout, or a new system rollout. If you do, make sure you are satisfied that the FCOO has experience with the particular kind of scenario on which you're about to embark.

Be clear about whether you need or expect them to physically work in your office or if the engagement will be fully remote, or some combination.

Next

If you run your business using the Entrepreneurial Operating System (EOS) management framework, then you want a Fractional Integrator as your FL, rather than a generalized FCOO. The next chapter will explain everything you need to know about FIs.

If your business does not run on EOS and marketing, sales, or operations are not your main pain points, and your main issues are financial, skip to Chapter 10: "Finance—How a Fractional Chief Financial Officer (FCFO) Makes You More Strategic and Increases Your Profits So You Stop Making Decisions in the Dark."

9.

EOS® Operations

How a Fractional Integrator Accelerates Massive Action for Companies Running on EOS

JIN AND KEVIN CHON, THE BROTHER AND SISTER CO-founders of Coop Home Goods, an e-commerce company, were self-implementing the EOS management framework. They were working incredibly hard and seeing success, but although they'd been using EOS tools for about a year, they felt like they were not really going all-in. They had the sense they weren't getting the full benefit.

So based on a colleague's referral, they brought in Jamie Munoz, an FI for companies running on EOS. Jin and Kevin regularly reiterate that Jamie's biggest value to them is her outside perspective. According to Jamie:

> They really, really appreciate me asking them the hard questions or the uncomfortable questions. The first quarter, we focused on starting to embed radical candor into the organization, meaning that we promoted being open and honest for the greater good of the business. Nothing to hurt anyone's feelings. It's

not personal. They asked me time and time again, what can we do to improve? How can we be better?

Jamie has seen how other businesses their size or bigger do things and she can guide them on best practices in business and in how to get maximum value by fully implementing the EOS tools. With tools like Quarterly Conversations™ between managers and direct reports, Same Page Meetings™, and tightly run and effective leadership team meetings, they have seen a huge change for the better.

Jin and Kevin, together with Jamie and the other members of the leadership team, decided on a major strategic shift due to the coronavirus pandemic and the related disruptions to manufacturing and distribution from China. They needed to diversify manufacturing and improve internal operations and logistics, but they knew they could not do this without someone with that kind of experience to become their full-time Integrator—that is, a COO.

Jamie assisted with a quarterly goal (Rock) to help them hire a full-time Integrator. They decided to use Titus Talent Strategies, a recruiting firm founded by Jonathan D. Reynolds, which itself runs on EOS, to help them find the right person for them. Jamie explained:

As a Fractional Integrator, the integrity is always to do what is best for the organization which sometimes means bringing in full-time talent when the time is right. Inevitably working ourselves out of jobs!

When the right Integrator starts, even if he or she has no EOS experience, Jin and Kevin want Jamie to mentor them into the role and teach them how EOS works, after which her engagement with the company will end happily and successfully.

Ich bin ein Fractional Integrator

The brand of Fractional Leadership I personally practice is that I am an FI (like an FCOO) for companies using the EOS management framework.

For context, businesses must have some "operating system" just like computers must have one. What does that mean? If you have a Windows computer, then it runs programs like PowerPoint, Excel, QuickBooks, and Zoom. But those programs run inside an operating system that makes the computer and all the programs on it run. Your product or service and your business processes are your "programs." The way your business works (or fails to work!) is your operating system.

There are a number of business operating systems out there, like Scaling-Up, 4DX, Pinnacle, and Business Made Simple. One of the most popular and successful ones is EOS. Over 10,000 companies around the world are running on EOS with Professional and Certified EOS Implementers® right now.

The main thing is not *which* specific operating system you use for your business but that you decide on and use only one. If you don't have some sort of operating system for your business, you're just working ad hoc. That works in the startup phase. In fact, I believe that adaptability and all-hands-on-deck, no structure approach is critical to survive the startup gauntlet which so many businesses don't even survive.

But when you get to be ten, twenty, thirty, or fifty people, you realize that this approach stops working. You hit the ceiling. This is when most businesses either reinvent the wheel by creating their own operating system or use an "out of the box" option, like EOS or one of the other operating systems mentioned above.

When I joined the healthcare startup in which I "grew up" entrepreneurially, I was the first full-time employee, even before the founder joined. He read the book *Traction: Get a Grip on Your Business* by Gino Wickman, the founder of EOS. He fell in love with Traction and EOS and ultimately retained one of the great Certified EOS Implementers, Jonathan B. Smith, to help us implement EOS.

Why did we do it? We planned to grow extremely quickly. Thankfully, we successfully achieved that goal and became the largest agency of our type in the entire state of New York in less than three years.

Even in those early days, we didn't want the wheels to fall off the bus, so to speak, when we began to grow quickly. So we implemented EOS to create the rails to keep our operations from falling apart when we started growing really fast. That helped keep us on track so that our vision, execution, processes, and team health kept pace with our growth.

Over the next couple of years, I built most of the operational divisions of the company and internally owned our implementation of EOS.

Where Do Fractional Integrators Come From?

As mentioned earlier, Gino Wickman and Mark C. Winters mentioned the FI concept in their book *Rocket Fuel: The One Essential Combination That Will Get You More of What You Want from Your Business*, which is all about the Visionary-Integrator relationship—that is, the relationship between the founder and a COO, general manager, or president. They explain:

> Rather than bite off the full-time salary of an experienced hire, you engage that same level of resource (or sometimes even more experienced) for less than a full-time arrangement…This can be a way to create immediate impact by adding much-needed capabilities that you are currently missing while softening the financial blow of biting off the full-time hire all at once.

I spoke with Gino Wickman for this book. He explained to me that ironically:

> I never intended for there to be Fractional Integrators. I strongly urge that focus be the first priority. You're better off having 100 percent of someone's attention, effort, and energy. They go to sleep thinking about you. They wake up thinking about you. But not every company can afford that focus. It's used in a situation when a company just can't afford the horsepower, but, beautifully, they can afford a fraction of that horsepower and get a lot of the benefit. Rick Wilson, Jerry Rick, and many others have built very successful Fractional Integrator businesses. So it works.

I personally believe FIs, like other kinds of FLs, became popular for the same reason Gino alludes to. When you can't scale without bringing on experienced executive leadership but can't afford that full-time help until after you've scaled or aren't quite ready for the commitment, you're in the jaws of that Entrepreneurial Catch-22. Bringing on an FI is your way through that until they can successfully get you ready to hire someone like themselves full-time.

Why Companies Engage with Fractional Integrators

Now that you understand some basic background about my own personal journey to become an FI and about EOS, let's explore the question, why do people retain FIs?

Rick Wilson, founder of The Integrator Group, whom many call the OG of FIs, says:

> EOS works. It often takes somebody in-house who knows how to use the tools properly, has used them before. I know what it looks like to win. I can invoke that with people and get them excited. That's why it's important to work myself out of the job. While I'm in there, I'm constantly working to get that into your head so I can move on and help someone else.

Rick shared with me how he began working with a husband and wife who had been implementing EOS for four years. They had twelve people in the company, and when he started working with them, he asked them for their Accountability Chart and V/TO. They couldn't produce anything but an out-of-date version from earlier in their journey.

He explains how the first thing he did with them, like with most of his clients, was to revisit and refresh their EOS tools so they could get the value they were meant to take from them. They had begun skipping Level 10 Meetings when a client meeting came up, never migrated EOS down below the leadership team level of the organization, and got upset with employees when they exhibited one of their "official" core values—fun. It turns out that their core values were more like PR statements than values coming from their core. There were multiple people in the organization who were not great at their jobs, but the owners never took any decisive action on this.

During his first quarter with the team, Rick helped them freshen up and make their EOS tools living documents. Well before the end of his first quarter with them, they had a handful of Rocks that really were important (not the excessive ten to fifteen Rocks they'd lazily set), revised their Accountability Chart to represent their true ideal structure, and made their V/TO into a vision document that really popped and motivated them.

By three quarters into his engagement with them, Rick had led them to let go of the people who were not "Right Person Right Seat" fits and hire several more people who were. They now have a strong leadership team they can rely on, they've migrated the EOS discipline into the entire organization, and they're ready to find a full-time Integrator.

What It Feels Like Now When You Don't Have a "Right Person Right Seat" Integrator

If you've grown big enough to require an Integrator, you, as the Visionary, are feeling overwhelmed because you must also fulfill the Integrator role. And because you love working on big deals, developing big relationships, and working at 30,000 feet, and hate day-to-day management and long-term follow-through, you and your team are feeling frustrated.

You're hitting the ceiling because you don't know how to increase sales, production is at capacity, and any new business just adds stress. You know you need an Integrator but can't afford to hire an experienced executive full-time.

An Integrator is someone who "integrates" all of the major functions of the business, serves as the glue that holds together the organization, ensures that "all the trains run on time," removes obstacles, and operates more from logic and a sense of follow-through. The Integrator focuses on leadership, management, and accountability, ensuring the execution of day-to-day operations of the business so the Visionary can work on the big stuff he or she enjoys the most and is best in the world at.

There are two types of organizations who need FIs and each one tracks very closely with the two general types of FCOOs I explained in the previous chapter: Doer Leaders and Manager Leaders.

Small Businesses (SBs) of five to twenty people, which are very often self-implementing EOS, usually seek out Doer Leader FIs. These organizations have a founder-Visionary who's also stuck in the Integrator seat and may have no one or just one other person on the leadership team. Such organizations seek out Doer Leader FIs who will do more than only perform the traditional Integrator role described above. They also need someone to personally get a lot of stuff done.

Midsize businesses (MSBs), typically twenty-plus people, require Manager Leader FIs. They need FIs who've run organizations like theirs or bigger to primarily focus on leading, managing, and creating accountability for the leadership team to act as a strategic leader and drive results.

Some businesses retain an FI even though they can afford someone full-time as an interim solution while they search for a full-time Integrator. Because they know the process can sometimes take six to eighteen months to find the right person, they don't want to suffer all that time without the benefit of having a Right Person Right Seat person in the Integrator role.

What a Typical Fractional Integrator Engagement Looks Like

FIs are similar to FCOOs in the ways they help their clients get aligned around the right structure, people, metrics, and processes. The difference is that they are experienced in using the same EOS tools you use for your business.

There are four major types of accountability for FIs.

Leading Your Level 10 Meetings™

The first typical element of an FI engagement is Leading your Level 10 (L10) Meetings. To the uninitiated, this can sound like an administrative function. But those who've experienced L10 Meetings with or without a good Integrator know that it is like night and day. It is the difference between an effective, action-oriented leadership team and an ineffective team.

Before I learned how to be a great L10 Meeting leader, here's what our leadership team meetings were like.

First, we didn't listen to a lot of the advice our Professional EOS Implementer gave us. We neglected to set minimum goals for each of the Measurables in our Scorecard. That's the first thing that would have been different with an effective FI.

When one of our Measurables was off-track, its owner would launch into a long explanation expounding on why it was off track. Again, this went against our EOS Implementer's teachings. Others would respond and the process would take five to ten minutes. The same thing happened when a second Measurable was off-track.

When it came time to report on whether our Rocks were on-track or off-track, it was the same story. The whole reporting section of the meeting was long, laborious, and interminable. It left us with very little time for solving our key issues.

When people did discuss issues throughout the Scorecard, Rock, and To-Do sections of the meeting, they end up talking about things in the order they just happened to come up in conversation, rather than based on what is actually important.

So what did we do to compensate? We extended our meetings to two or two and a half painful, tortuous, and largely unproductive hours. Meetings took over our days, we dreaded them, and they ate our other important priorities for lunch.

Can you relate?

The primary value of the L10 Meeting agenda is that it forces you to be intentional about how to most effectively use the leadership team's time. It does this by forcing you to simply smoke out your issues when Measurables or Rocks are off-track and simply drop them down to the Issues List without discussion right then. It makes leadership meetings tight, brief, and wickedly effective.

Now when I start leading my clients' L10 Meetings as an FI, they tell me that the team immediately begins getting far more done in much less time. This is because FIs run L10 Meetings like friendly drill sergeants. Nice but no nonsense. I cut off discussion in the reporting section and drop down far more issues to the Issues List than they were accustomed to. Far from stymieing discussion, this allows the team to be intentional about what they discuss and solve.

The other main difference is that my clients report solving many more issues and with much more concrete To-Dos than they used to. Whereas they may have talked around and around two or three issues per meeting before, after a few weeks, my leadership teams sometimes solve six, nine, or even twelve issues in a single L10 Meeting, all without feeling rushed. It's all about focus.

Participate in Same Page Meetings™

The second main accountability for FIs is participating in the meetings EOS recommends between Visionaries and Integrators, called Same Page Meetings. Because FIs are not with you full-time, I like to do these just about every week. But that is something that you will work out with your FI depending on what feels right for you.

Same Page Meetings allow you, as Visionary, to get a deeper pulse on what's happening in their own business from your FI. They also give you someone to talk through your newest ideas and what's on your mind or annoying you with someone who's been there and built a business your size or larger before. It also creates a forum and trusted advisor with whom to discuss and solve issues related to the members of your leadership team.

Rock or Leadership Team Support

This third area of accountability is more miscellaneous. It depends on the needs of the client. FIs may meet with the members of your leadership team weekly to help train them in the habits of accountability so that they get and keep their Rocks, Measurables, and To-Dos on-track.

Alternatively, they may personally take on a Rock like documenting a core process or driving the hiring of a much-needed manager or leadership team position. Business owners sometimes need FIs to assist, mentor, and coach the members of the leadership team on issues they encounter or how to tackle challenges they haven't been exposed to before.

Participate in Sessions with the EOS Implementer

The fourth and final common area of accountability is participation in your full-day sessions with your EOS Implementer— your Quarterlies and two-day Annual Planning sessions. As the Integrator of the leadership team, your FI participates in your EOS sessions to give your team the benefit of his or her knowledge and expertise as you and your team resolve the team's most critical issues, decide on your next set of Rocks, and reexamine, refine, and realign around your Accountability Chart and V/TO.

Time Commitment and Cost

This is very dependent on whether you're looking for a Doer Leader FI or Manager Leader FI, as described above.

Business owners tend to engage Doer Leader FIs for more time each week, typically between one to two and a half days per week for costs ranging from $100–$150 per hour or $4,000–$5,000 per month for one day per week or $10,000–$12,500 per month for two and a half days per week.

Manager Leader FIs typically work with their clients about one day per week, although some work with them half a day each week and others do somewhat more. They typically charge in the range of $6,000–$13,000 each month per day of the week committed.

What to Ask Potential Fractional Integrators

Before choosing an FI, ask yourself whether you need a Doer Leader or a Manager Leader. This will give you greater clarity when communicating your needs to potential FIs and ensure that your expectations are aligned with theirs.

Ask whether the FI has the kind of industry experience or situational experience you require. For instance, if you need someone with manufacturing experience to avoid a too-long learning curve, make sure your potential FI has it.

As with any FL, communicate your desired outcomes from the engagement before it begins and ensure that they are on the same page with you.

Confirm that the potential FI has actual experience as an Integrator, not just a departmental leader or project manager. Many people aspire to be FIs based on a high Integrator score on Mark C. Winters's excellent Crystallizer Assessment but do not yet have practical Integrator experience. Unfortunately, I have seen such engagements end in frustration and disappointment because the FI lacks real-life experience operating a company of the client's scale.

Next

If you're good-to-go for now when it comes to marketing, sales, and operations, the next area we'll consider is help with the finance component of your organization using a Fractional Chief Financial Officer.

10.

Finance

How a Fractional Chief Financial Officer (FCFO) Makes You More Strategic and Increases Your Profits
BECAUSE YOU DON'T KNOW WHAT YOU DON'T KNOW, FLs can help you solve problems you didn't even know you had.

Tom is the CEO and majority owner of McAndrew Inc., a manufacturing business that makes products found in big-box retailers around the country. It's a family business created by Tom's great-grandfather based outside of Detroit, Michigan. Tom originally reached out to FocusCFO to drill down into some major gross margin issues they were having.[32]

As David Bourke, FocusCFO's Director of CFO Support explained, "We sent one of our CFOs, Danielle, who had deep financial leadership experience at other manufacturing businesses, to McAndrew to work with them about two days per week."

Tom and the company's controller met with Danielle. The controller explained how the company needed help getting their gross margin data in check. It was completely

---

32 All identifying information in this case study has been changed to preserve anonymity.

inconsistent. A certain product would be 15 percent one month and 40 percent another month. They needed someone to get to the bottom of it and fix the issue.

Tom then excused himself because he had to go into another meeting. Shortly after he left the room, the controller confided in Danielle that they needed help with more than just their gross margin data. There was a bigger issue—a much bigger issue. It was Tom, the CEO, himself.

As Danielle got started, Tom wasn't around much because he traveled frequently for sales and business development. While he was away, she took the opportunity to meet individually with the entire leadership team and a few other key employees. Danielle immediately began to see a pattern emerge during these conversations. No one was stepping up fully in their own leadership roles because there was a fear culture within the company.

Danielle asked the president what he thought was going on. Why were people afraid to take ownership of decisions? His answer was, "We have lost at least five key people in the past few years. Some were asked to leave, and some left before they were axed. Today, people are afraid to step up and take a stand on critical issues out of fear."

Deeper into the conversations, Danielle learned that the CEO had fired one person after another when they said something he didn't like. No one was willing to make constructive suggestions or take any risks because they were concerned that they would be the next one fired.

The fear culture went all the way down into the production facility. Everyone kept their head down and barely greeted each other. Mid-level managers were afraid of having their heads bitten off by the CEO or losing their jobs. So they took out their frustrations on frontline employees when things were not perfect, which only served to perpetuate the culture of fear.

It also became clear that finance was not the only aimless department. The entire organization lacked clear priorities. People only reacted to problems. They felt like they were running around and around in circles and not getting anywhere.

For example, the CEO announced one day that he had ordered a production line for a new product without talking with either the production team or his leadership team. He just went out and ordered it and said it was going to be the best in the industry. Fast forward to several months after the line was in. It was running at only 15–20 percent capacity and was a total flop. It was part of a never-ending cycle where none of the CEO's new ideas had ever achieved the desired outcome.

By the time Tom returned from his trip, Danielle had prepared a game plan for getting McAndrew into a much stronger financial position, decreasing its debt load, fixing its gross margin inconsistency issues, and putting the company in a position for more growth and more profit.

When Danielle sat down with Tom, she told him:

> I want to get your take on my plan to help to get the company in a better position, but I want to say something first about some deeper issues for a couple of minutes. If we are on the same page with what I am about to share with you, then great. But if we are not on the same page, then I don't think there is anything I can do to help you on the financial side. Because as Peter Drucker says, "Culture eats strategy for breakfast," and I cannot be successful on the financial side if we don't fix the culture.

Tom heard her out and took her somewhat by surprise in his openness to her frank feedback. Danielle offered some suggestions for how they could fix the culture, and how to get more focused on fully executing McAndrew's top priorities.

The CEO's response was, "Those are some big changes. How can we get the team to accept you and adopt those radical adjustments?" Little did he know how much the leadership team was already counting on Danielle to fix the bigger issues.

Danielle worked with Tom to come up with an email to introduce her to the team in her new role as their FCFO and explain the proposed changes to the team, which Tom sent out. He was pleasantly surprised by the team's openness and acceptance.

One of the big changes Danielle brought to the table was for McAndrew to implement EOS, the Entrepreneurial Operating System framework for running a business. This would allow the leadership team to get laser-focused on their priorities. Running EOS would help bring accountability to the company by identifying roles and responsibilities for all personnel and give them a common language and methodology to start communicating more openly and honestly in a safe environment. They brought in an EOS Implementer to help them do that.

Danielle also began tackling the gross margin issue. The ERP and general ledger systems did not fully align. She led the team to resolve that problem.

She then instituted a capital committee, which they had never had before. They now have a one-year and three-year capital plan and no longer make significant capital improvement investments without discussing the changes with the leadership team and understanding exactly how and why they would be a great benefit to the company.

McAndrew's leadership team, under Danielle's direction, also implemented a budgeting process that involved the entire leadership team in making key strategic decisions. The controller was no longer tasked with formulating a budget alone, in a vacuum. Everyone from the leadership team had to participate in the company's annual plan. Now they all had a feeling of ownership, like they were stakeholders in McAndrew's priorities and strategic plans.

Danielle also implemented a quarterly meeting with McAndrew's banker. She told the team that it was important to share everything the business was doing, how they were improving their management system with EOS, and the results they were seeing with their banker. Danielle explained to the leadership team that it was important to share this information to foster a real relationship with their banker and not allow their dealings to remain purely transactional. When tough times inevitably arrive, they need their banker to really understand their business and their plan.

Now, a year and half later, McAndrew has continued to focus on reducing its debt to a healthy level. The company is executing and profiting from the new efforts initiated by Danielle, which were part of a conscious, intentional strategic plan.

They've let go of one leadership team member who was not open to the new approach and culture and have brought in two other people from outside the company. Danielle's fresh insights have been eye-opening for the leadership team. Everyone is now taking more ownership over their roles, and Tom now feels freer to focus on what he loves doing—big sales and relationship building. The company is stronger and healthier now because of all the changes and the leadership Danielle provided.

As an FCFO, Danielle wasn't afraid to have the tough conversation with Tom. Nothing happens overnight, but the greater openness and lower fear level is now migrating down from the leadership team into middle management and among the frontline workers. Danielle is grateful to be part of such a great team.

What's Happening That's Making You Even Think of Hiring an FCFO?

There are two main scenarios that may be causing you to consider engaging the help of an FCFO. The first is simply that the person who grew up with the company handling finance is somewhat out of his or her element at your current scale.

Your head of finance is someone who's not a professional CFO with experience advising and analyzing the needs and unique decision points of a multimillion-dollar venture. They may have learned finance through taking courses, bookkeeping training, YouTube videos, or perhaps they have CPA or controller experience.

The second scenario is that you're facing a specific finance-related crisis, challenge, or transaction, such as facing a cash crunch, experiencing low or negative profit margin, suffering from high expenses, outgrowing your finance systems, navigating an audit, raising capital, or preparing for a sale or acquisition.

In either case, your revenue might be between $2 million and $50 million and you recognize that your leadership team lacks the financial experience and expertise you need at this stage.

How Does an FCFO Engagement Work?

FCFOs are the earliest adopted and most widely known type of FLs. Why is that? Perhaps it is because financial information is more standardized. Also, people may feel that because businesses face a smaller number of *types* of financial challenges, they more easily understand how an outsider can quickly understand and advise them on what to do.

Because the FCFO field thrived earlier than other types of Fractional Leadership, there are more solo practitioner and organizational Fractional Leadership (OFL) FCFO firms than other types of FLs available to you.

Janet[33] founded a business selling refurbished computer hardware. Fighting tooth and nail, she grew the business to $1.5 million in revenue, but she was generating about $50,000 per year in profit, before her meager salary. It seemed that no matter how hard she worked, the business never grew.

As Steve from the FocusCFO team started working with her, he walked through her warehouse, met her customer sales team, and talked about the business and how it worked. Janet was proud of her accounting reports and the level of detail she tracked and how that helped her manage her costs.

Steve looked at Janet's reports and finally asked her, "So how do you know if you've had a really good day?" His question caught her off guard. She had never been asked that before. She sat back in her chair, glanced out the window, and then finally said, "Well, if we sell over $10,000 worth of product, and our margin on what we sold that day is over 40 percent, and we don't have any inventory on hand that is more than sixty days old, then that's a good day." Steve pushed

---

33 All names have been changed to preserve anonymity.

the accounting reports aside and said to Janet, "That's how we are going to run the business. Every day, we are going to try to hit those three benchmarks."

Fast forward three years later. Janet's business did over $3 million of sales and had a pretax income of almost $400,000 by focusing exclusively on those three metrics.

Because you don't know what you don't know, FLs can help you solve problems you didn't even know you had.

Like other types of FLs, in the initial stages of an engagement, your FCFO will likely spend time talking with you and your leadership team to understand your business, revenue model, goals, dreams, and plans for the future. He or she will certainly review financial data as well.

Most importantly, your FCFO will become a trusted member of your leadership team, whether he or she is with you once a month or every week. They'll become a strategic advisor on your leadership team's decisions that touch finance—that is, almost all of them.

Depending on the state of your financial data, they'll "clean up" your books, if necessary, with the help of your bookkeeper(s) or an outside bookkeeping service.

Your FCFO will look at your Accounts Receivable (collections) and Accounts Payable processes and find improvements or efficiencies based on their significant experience. You could be leaving money on the table or paying your vendors too quickly, which is bad for cash flow. As they say, cash is king.

Depending on the mandate you agreed on with your FCFO, they will likely oversee your bookkeeping, accounting, insurance, banking, tax, and legal functions to ensure that you're managing your risk and that you're covered from all angles.

FCFOs often find that people need updated, augmented, or new financial technology systems to get financially healthy. They will ensure that these systems are integrated with marketing, sales, and operations. They will oversee this process so you'll be in a better position when their engagement is complete than you were when they started.

They will take over your financial reporting so you and the other members of the leadership team have the data you need to make great decisions. This includes the all-important budgeting process. Approximately 50 percent of businesses close within their first five years of existence. You don't want to become one of those because you spent more than you could afford, ran out of cash, and couldn't make payroll.

Most FCFOs do not want to permanently embed themselves into your organization. They want to get your ducks in a row, financially speaking, so your business can become healthier and you can thrive and focus on what your business *really* does for its customers or clients.

Once your organization is healthier and has the tools and practices it needs to scale successfully, they will stay with you until you're ready for them to help level up someone internally to take on the CFO or Head of Finance role or to help you hire a full-time CFO.

Coronavirus, Lockdowns, and Cash Crunches, Oh My!

Kevin McMahon, an FCFO with Vertex Advisors, helped lead several organizations through the coronavirus-related lockdowns and the related financial crunch. After the dust settled a couple of months in, most of his clients did relatively well compared to many and actually needed to go on a hiring spree.

It's a good problem to have, but Kevin knew that they could easily get ahead of themselves and end up obligating themselves to more in payroll and other high fixed-cost expenses than revenue they had coming in—the dreaded cash crunch.

Two of his clients were in the biotech space. Because they could not even hope to predict their upcoming revenue back in March and April of 2020, he advised them to implement a hiring freeze. Because Kevin knew how to look at the data and start or refreeze hiring with confidence, once the revenue and operational data for the first couple of months post-COVID came in, he had the information he needed to create financial triggers for hiring.

For example, he told one company that if they hit X number of lab tests per month, they could hire two additional lab technicians. He created triggers like this for all the positions they needed to hire, thus enabling them to hire with confidence. They did not have to make decisions in the dark.

Accountant or FCFO?

It is sometimes unclear to people when they need an FCFO versus when to simply call their accountant.

You should call a public accountant when your main needs are tax and financial-legal-related advice. You need an FCFO when you need operations-meets-finance strategic leadership.

If you need more episodic tax or financial advice, call your accountant. When you need help leading the execution of an internal financial overhaul or ongoing financial leadership from someone who can embed themselves more deeply than an accountant can and understands from experience running a business how to marry financial wisdom with operations, you need an FCFO.

What to Ask Potential FCFOs before Starting

If you are retaining an FCFO because of a specific transactional need or type of crisis like an M&A transaction, due diligence, bankruptcy, restructuring, or cash crisis, you definitely want to ensure they have proven experience with that kind of scenario.

Ensure that your potential FCFO has full-time CFO experience before they "went fractional." Like other kinds of FLs, people must have first gone through the gauntlet of deep CFO service with an organization to earn the chops necessary to spot issues quickly and find solutions in a fractional scenario.

If the learning curve for your business model is great, ensure that the potential FCFOs you're speaking with have industry experience. For example, if you have a home care business that bills Medicaid payors and you need someone who understands that industry so they're not starting from scratch, make sure that background is there before either of you waste your time.

Time Commitment and Cost

Some FCFOs work with their clients half a day each month, others spend two half days per month with their clients, and still others spend one day per week with them. This varies greatly depending on the client's needs.

Rates range from an hourly rate of $185–$300 per hour to monthly retainers starting at $2,500 for one day per month (or two half days) and up to $12,000 for one day per week.

Next

Let's say that your marketing, sales, operations, and finance components are doing great, or at least well enough. If your greatest need or what's keeping you up at night relates to the proprietary tech products or systems you built and that you sell to your customers, or if you need your out-of-the-box systems up and running every second for your business to run, you may need a Chief Technology Officer or Fractional Chief Information Officer.

The next chapter will explain the basics of what each one does, how they differ, and how to determine when you need them versus when you can use a consultant or can rely on your Managed Services Provider.

11.

Technology

How to Leverage a Fractional Chief Information
Officer (FCIO) or Fractional Chief Technology
Officer (FCTO) When You Can't Afford One
Second of Downtime

VIKTOR[34] WAS CHARGED WITH LEADING ENVIRONMENTAL
cleanup firm Crystal Cleanup Corp after their spinoff from a
much larger organization. The challenge was that their entire
IT infrastructure, including servers, phones, computers, email
systems, ERP, and security were remaining with their former
parent company.

Aside from running the newly created company, building its client base, and overseeing the acquisition of smaller
environmental cleanup companies, Viktor also had to create
Crystal's full IT infrastructure *from scratch*. All he had to work
with were four technicians and one software developer. The
parent company was not giving up any of its senior technology leadership.

---

34 All identifying information regarding Viktor's company has been changed to protect
anonymity.

Based on a recommendation from friends, Viktor found Chris Coluccio, CEO of Techworks Consulting, and retained him and his firm as FCIO to lead Crystal Cleanup's IT setup and buildup, with the goal of eventually setting up Crystal Cleanup to operate independently.

During the following months, Chris took Crystal Cleanup through a step-by-step setup of each key element of the IT infrastructure, including ITIL standards, a ticketing system, processes for working between time zones, phone systems, local and remote data centers with their own rackspace, security systems, and individual workstations.

As head of Crystal's IT operations, he and his team set up tagging and monitoring systems and established processes and procedures, including meeting and accountability processes, training, and standardized hardware and operating systems at every level, from companywide down to every single device.

Chris set up such standardized, simplified, and cookie-cutter processes and systems that integrating the other companies Crystal purchased became a relative breeze. Instead of the months-long painful process, each acquiree's systems integrated in Crystal's in a matter of weeks.

During the four years following Crystal's spinoff from its parent company, under Chris's leadership as FCIO, he and his team trained Crystal's entire staff, hired a global IT director and other necessary employees, set up all of their back-end systems, and set up their meeting and accountability processes.

As Richard Bach said, "If you love someone, set them free." After a little over four years setting up Crystal's IT infrastructure, team, and processes, Chris helped them become fully independent and self-sustaining.

That is the power of bringing Fractional technology leadership into your organization. You can get the leadership, experience, and resources of a $300,000 executive for a fraction of the rollout time and cost.

What Things Look Like Before

Let me start by painting a picture of who likely *doesn't* need an FCIO or FCTO.

If you're like most (regular) service, retail, manufacturing, or professional services businesses, you certainly depend heavily on technology, but you didn't create that technology yourself or don't have such a customized or complicated set of systems that you need anything beyond a great Managed Services Provider (MSP) and/or consultant or two to keep things running smoothly.

If, however, you have a customized or complex system of bought-software (including cloud-based) or you've built the technology your business literally needs at every second to serve its clients, then you may need an FCIO or FCTO.

Let's paint a picture of what that looks like.

You or a member of your leadership team are doing your best to manage a patchwork of freelancers, an MSP, a VoIP provider, and internal or external developers or resources, but you don't have the time, experience, or resources to do this well. It's taking a toll on your ability to do what you need in other parts of the business. It's holding you back.

Alternatively, you built a product using freelancers and you sell usage of that product to your customers. But you've now grown the business big enough that the product and your customers' needs are outgrowing your ability to serve them effectively. You're one outage or bug away from disaster.

Another scenario is that you need to do a technology-heavy rehaul or turnaround of your operations, but you're not sure where to start and certainly don't have the bandwidth to drive and oversee the months-long process. Neither does anyone on your team.

Do You Need an MSP, Technology Consultant, Process Consultant, or an FCIO or FCTO?

Virtually every business, and certainly one in growth mode, requires technology, including hardware, networking, security, internet, VoIP, and various Customer Relationship Management (CRM) software or Enterprise Resource Planning (ERP) systems to run day-to-day business.

According to Bill Abram, an FCIO and EOS Implementer, most organizations with under 1,000 employees need only a good MSP and VoIP company to succeed. Certainly, you need someone internally to take ownership of the results and find a new provider if things are not going well. But you don't need an FCIO or FCTO.

So Who Does Need an FCIO or FCTO?

FCTO. If you developed your own proprietary technology and have an internal or external development team maintaining it, you may need a full-time CTO or an FCTO. Without the right person focused on your product and the systems on which it operates, your entire business sits on very precarious ground.

You need someone who understands the servers on which those systems run, whether server-based or cloud-based. Your critical risks include data security, server reliability and speed, redundancy if something goes wrong, external and internal tampering, and hacking. You likely need someone with experience to take ownership over your technology.

FCIO. Even if you utilize others' technology, CRM, or ERP, if you're over 1,000 people, or have very complex, customized, or temperamental systems you desperately rely on every second, you may need an FCIO to allow you to sleep at night. You'll also free yourself up to focus on running and growing your business once your technology isn't hogging a huge share of your mental and emotional bandwidth.

Technology and Process Consultants. When do you need a technology or process consultant? In short, these professionals are most helpful when your need is more transactional or short term. If you need to choose and customize a technology once, a consultant can help you map out your business processes, research and choose the right technology solution for you to buy, and then hand off oversight of the actual implementation to someone internally.

Many technology and process consultants also offer implementation services. This still falls under the transactional or short-term umbrella. This means that they'll oversee the selection, execution, data migration, and rollout of the selected technology so that you don't have to. But after that, their work is done.

If you'll have significant ongoing needs that require strategic, ongoing leadership to oversee and/or continue improving and iterating the technologies on which you rely, then you should consider retaining an FCIO or FCTO.

What's the Difference between an FCIO versus an FCTO?

Put simply, Burke Autrey, CEO of Fortium Partners, the largest FCIO and FCTO firm, with about 115 FLs as of this writing, explains that you need an FCIO when you're a buyer of technology and an FCTO when you're a builder of technology.

Another way of looking at it is that you need an FCTO when you sell usage of the technology you built to your customers and an FCIO when you're simply relying, even heavily, on someone else's technology to facilitate your delivery of a product or service not inherently related to that technology.

Burke explains that a "CIO primarily oversees operational or the buying of technology and solving complementing enterprise problems with the technology."

On the other hand, he says that an FCTO is for a "company that's primarily selling technology. Most of their revenue comes from the sale of technology…The FCTO is well versed in product management, product development, security, developer operations, and hosting products that are for sale."

FCIO and FCTO Firms versus Solo Practitioners

Review the section on Organizational Fractional Leaders (OFLs) versus solo entrepreneur FLs in Chapter 3, "What Fractional Leadership Engagements Look Like So You Know Exactly What to Expect." There are a number of technology OFLs like Fortium Partners, led by Burke Autrey, among others.

One advantage of OFLs specific to technology is when you have a hybrid need for more than one type of FL. For instance, let's say you need a CIO a half day each week and a CTO one and a half days per week. A single OFL can provide you with both. That is aside from the fact that the OFL takes responsibility for the engagement so that if one particular FL is not a fit, they can provide you with another person.

Burke relates how he placed both a CIO and CTO with a healthcare client simultaneously to help them achieve some ambitious compliance-related and tech rollout goals in a limited period of time. They successfully ended the engagement by helping their client not only achieve those goals but also find and transition technology operations over to a permanent, full-time CIO.

There are many solo practitioner FCIOs and FCTOs throughout the world as well. For some business owners, the individual person, their independence, or their often somewhat lower price point make them a more attractive option.

What the Engagement Looks Like

The order of operations at the beginning of an FCIO or FCTO engagement depends heavily on why the business brings them in. Things look different if they're there to implement a herculean technology overhaul or to significantly level up and then shepherd ongoing operations.

They'll likely start off getting a lay of the land by getting to know you and the internal or external technology people you already have in place, and by exploring the systems you already have. They will work with you and your team members to understand your business model and legal or regulatory framework. Finally, they will learn from you about your long-term plans, vision, and goals.

This groundwork is critical for an FCIO or FCTO to ensure that your technology serves you not only in the short term, but so that they have the information necessary to create a roadmap for the future to ensure that your systems continue to align with and support the achievement of your goals and don't become an obstacle or liability later on.

Once they have the lay of the land and understand your ultimate destination, your FCIO or FCTO will prioritize the next steps necessary to align your systems with your current and ultimately future business.

On an ongoing basis, an FCIO or FCTO is your partner and continual resource in driving, overseeing, adapting, and iterating your technology infrastructure or products so that you can sleep at night and focus on growing the other parts of your business. You can rest assured that someone who knows exactly what they're doing is taking care of the technology side of things.

Critically, this technology leader is a strategic partner and participates with your leadership team in their regular meetings and discussions. Ongoing operations, issue solving, budget, and future plans all touch your tech in some way. You want your FCIO or FCTO to hear and be aligned with the other parts of your organization. The rest of the team need your technology leader's input when it comes to day-to-day operations, financial decision making, and planning for the future.

Time Commitment and Cost

Similar to other types of FLs, FCIOs and FCTOs may spend two half days per month, half a day per week, or one day per week or more with you. This depends on your needs and, especially for CTOs managing an intense development process and team, may be even longer, like one and a half or two days per week.

Hourly rates, for those who use them, range from $100–$250 per hour. And monthly retainers range from $2,500–$15,000 depending on the FCIO's or FCTO's experience as well as the local market.

What to Ask Potential FCIOs and FCTOs

First, you must ensure that you and your potential FCIO or FCTO speak the same language. What do I mean? There are many terms that different people use and they don't always use them consistently.

People use terms like CIO, CTO, Head of Product, Product Manager, and Chief Information and Security Officer (CISO). They all mean different things and not everyone defines them the same way. So ask your potential FCIO or FCTO what they mean by those terms and confirm that you're both talking about the same things.

As always, communicate exactly what you want the engagement to achieve and in what time frame. Ensure that your potential FCIO or FCTO is on the same page with you and give them the opportunity to either communicate why you should tweak those goals or why they feel confident they can achieve them. Either way, your conversation will get you on the same page so you can decide whether the two of you are a fit.

Ensure that they have relevant, demonstrated experience doing something similar to what you need, particularly if your potential FCIO or FCTO has a daunting technology goal like overseeing a major new system rollout and data migration or directing the development of a product for sale to your customers.

If you're someone who naturally feels comfortable asking direct, probing questions, that's great. But even if you're someone for whom this doesn't come naturally, just remember that this is your business and that your most important goals are at stake. It's better to find out now whether the FL you're considering using has the knowledge and experience to drive the outcomes you need and want.

Ensure that your prospective FCIO or FCTO has industry experience if that is important. Examples include when your industry has an unusually specialized business model, complicated regulations that affect technology (like hospital systems or Department of Defense security requirements), or standards that would make the learning curve of someone without that industry experience unwieldy.

Next

We have now introduced the basics of what Fractional Leadership is, how it works, how to find the right FL, how to set up the engagement for success, and how, at a high level, Fractional Leadership works specifically for marketing, sales, operations, finance, and technology.

That concludes Part II of this book. In Part III, I take out my crystal ball and discuss the future of Fractional Leadership and consolidate the resources and questions I shared throughout this book into several brief checklists and questionnaires you can use to determine whether you're a good candidate for Fractional Leadership, what kind of FL you need, and how to find the right FL for you. I also include resources for where to find the right FL for you, how to set up the engagement with your chosen FL for success, and a sample Fractional Leadership agreement.

Part III

Bringing It All Together

12.

Wrap-Up

The Future of Fractional Leadership

Fractional Leadership is going to get more common. There is no data available on small and midsize business owners' awareness of the Fractional Leadership model, but based on anecdotal experience, it is growing.

I believe that this growth trajectory, even after the dust has settled in the post-coronavirus world, will continue. The genie is out of the bottle. The cat is out of the bag. And the beans have (fortunately) been spilled.

Mikey Likes It!

Like the old Life cereal commercial, many people didn't want to try Fractional Leadership before the lockdowns. They waited for the Mikeys of the world, who would try literally anything, to experiment with it first.

They could not understand how someone who was not with them full-time could serve as an effective leader or hold people they didn't work with every day accountable. They could not understand how someone working remotely could understand their business or oversee a team they couldn't see in person. Go back and read Chapter 3, "What Fractional Leadership Engagements Look Like So You Know Exactly What to Expect" for a more in-depth explanation of these issues.

Coronavirus and the associated lockdowns forced everyone and their friend to become Mikey and try out things they would have never attempted before. This greatly sped up the already-accelerating adoption of Fractional Leadership.

Business owners who had never considered using the remote work model, much less at the leadership level of their organizations, were forced to acclimate to it. Some will revert to their allergy to remote work, at least at the leadership level. But many others realized that once they got used to it, working together remotely was not as bad as they expected, and it even helped them offer more flexibility and access previously unattainable talent by people who don't live near them.

Although many FLs work with their clients in-person, much of the growth of Fractional Leadership is related to the statistical fact that it is much easier to find the right FL for you if you're not limited to people who live within a few miles of your business.

Less Is More

Although small businesses are always under pressure to do more with less and achieve great things on a shoestring budget, this became doubly true in the post-coronavirus world. Chaos reigned, social upheaval surged, and political tensions exploded. Uncertainty was everywhere.

Because of that new reality, people now don't want to lose their shirts knowing that the next crisis could be around the corner. When they don't have an experienced executive on their team and can't yet afford to hire someone like that full-time or aren't yet ready to commit to it, using an FL is the perfect way to jump-start their growth. It allows them to overcome their blockage without the lead time, commitment, or cost of a full-time C-level executive.

The Technological Event Horizon

Although not all FLs serve their clients remotely, more and more are. The increased security and effectiveness of the Google Workspace apps, Slack, Microsoft 365, Zoom, and the like have made it easier than ever before to work together from anywhere. It was possible before, but the tools have become more user-friendly. Because of their wide acceptance, almost everyone is already familiar with them, so it's easy to collaborate with new people at any time.

Some people have worked remotely for over one hundred years—certainly before coronavirus. According to *The Power Broker: Robert Moses and the Fall of New York* by Robert A. Caro, in the 1920s, Robert Moses built parks and parkways throughout New York State mostly via remote work.

Mr. Moses directed that two cars pick him up at home early every morning. He got into one car with his secretary as they drove to the first job site of the day. The second car followed behind them. He handed her all the notes and memos he had handwritten the night before and told her all of the decisions and instructions he needed to communicate to his team while she took copious notes.

At the job site, his secretary would get out of the car with all the memos and her notes and get into the second car which had been following them the whole way. She headed back to the office at opening time to disseminate all the memos, decisions, and directions communicated to her during her in-transit meeting that morning.

Although remote work was not invented in 2020, it became far easier and more common. I personally doubt whether, if the pandemic had happened twenty years earlier, in 2000, it would have had as great an impact on the prevalence of remote work in general and Fractional Leadership in particular.

"Going Fractional"

Many people, including C-level executives, are simply not wired for the risk involved in venturing out on their own, finding clients, and running their own business even though busy FLs make more than full-time executives. But many executives, particularly those working in entrepreneurial companies who have been bitten by the entrepreneurial bug, find it easier to branch out on their own.

One major challenge for potential FLs is how to leave a relatively safe job when they have families to support. In my experience, most people who "go fractional" either wait until they have a client or two to begin, perhaps having even started doing Fractional Leadership work as a side hustle, or have at least one client lined up before leaving their full-time jobs.

The truth is that no job is truly safe. People go from 100 percent income to 0 percent in one day if the company fires them or fails. All of their eggs are in one basket. Fractional Leadership at least allows its practitioners to balance their risk among several clients once they get off the ground. So in that sense, it is a safer option. The trick is bridging the gap between full-time work and a full client load.

Coronavirus and the associated lockdowns showed people what it was like to work more independently and remotely, even if they still excelled at their full-time positions. It made people more open to the side hustles many use as stepping-stones to taking the leap into Fractional Leadership.

The Future

As more and more people have used FLs, particularly post-coronavirus, they will tell their friends about it. That story will repeat itself. And as full-time work becomes less attractive to more executives, I believe that both sides of the Fractional Leadership equation will grow in relative balance with each other over the next several years.

Conclusion

WE HAVE TALKED ABOUT WHAT FRACTIONAL LEADERSHIP is and how business owners use FLs to leverage experienced C-level leaders to help them to break through the ceilings they couldn't figure out how to get past.

We've spoken about how business owners can determine whether Fractional Leadership is right for them, what kind of FL they need, how to find the right FL, and how to set up the engagement for success before it starts.

Finally, I described, at a high level, how each of the most common types of Fractional Leadership (marketing, sales, operations, finance, and technology) work, important factors to ask about or consider for each type, and I've made some predictions about the future of Fractional Leadership.

The next chapter contains questionnaires, checklists, and other resources consolidated into one place from throughout this book to make it easier for you to get clarity around whether Fractional Leadership is right for you, what kind of FL you need, how to find potential FLs, how to vet a potential FL's references, and how to set up an FL engagement for success.

If you're a business owner or member of an entrepreneurial leadership team interested in exploring Fractional Leadership, happy hunting!

I hope this book has been a great resource for you. For more information and to stay connected with me and others who are interested, visit www.FractionalLeadership.io. There, you can subscribe to my email newsletter, find *Win Win* podcast interviews with guests who'll teach you things you didn't know, and a blog with articles and news for all things related to Fractional Leadership.

Resources

Questions and Resources to Find Your Ideal Fractional Leader and Set Up the Engagement for Success

For more context and information about these questions and resources, please read the relevant chapters earlier in this book.

Five Questions to Determine Whether You're a Good Candidate for FL

1. Are you looking for (a) leadership, strategy, management, and someone to drive accountability? Or (b) someone who can personally get a lot of stuff done?

2. Do you (a) already have one or more members of your leadership team participating remotely? Or (b) is there a strong culture of the leadership team being physically together in one office all of the time?

3. Are you someone who (a) can get comfortable trusting and listening to someone who's not in your business full-time, who learns to understand it at a high level with a deep knowledge of similar businesses? Or (b) do you know you'll never be able to trust, listen to, or respect the opinion and guidance of someone who is not there full-time?

4. Will you, as the business owner, (a) truly commit to reinforce the FL's role and any new processes or procedures with their team? Or (b) will you often allow circumvention of the new process or procedures or initiate or allow end runs around the FL?

5. Can you (a) afford 30–50 percent of the cost of an experienced full-time executive? Or (b) is that level of compensation for an FL beyond your business's financial means?

If you answer "(a)" more often than "(b)," you may be a good candidate for Fractional Leadership. If not, your best bet may be a full-time hire, consultant, freelancer, or continuing to do your best until you can hire the kind of experienced C-level executive you need full-time. Check out my suggestions in Chapter 4, "How to Figure Out Whether You're a Candidate for Fractional Leadership" for more information on those alternatives.

Two Questions to Determine Which Type of FL You Need First/Most

1. What part of your business is your greatest pain point— marketing, sales, operations, finance, or technology?

2. Is that the underlying problem or merely a symptom?

Fractional Leader Referral Resources

www.FractionalLeadership.io

This is my vetted FL referral platform to help you find the right FL for marketing, sales, operations (both FCOO and Fractional Integrator), finance, and technology.

When I was on the client side searching for an FL (and on the FL side meeting potential clients), the hardest thing I found was the long, laborious, manual process of finding the right FL.

I had to manually explore a completely nonstandardized set of individual FL websites to try and tease out whether they had the industry or situational experience we needed, where they were located, and what they charged. And even then, I ended up having calls with people or firms who weren't in our price range; if we needed someone near our home base to come in in-person, I had to ask many of them individually where they were located.

I created www.FractionalLeadership.io as a vetted FL referral platform because it is what I wished I had whenever I needed to find the right FL for a client.

The "Matchmaking" section of my website eliminates the manual work and allows you to skip straight to the finalists. It does this by profiling FLs for industry experience, situational expertise, rates, and several other factors. My team has conducted probing reference checks with at least three of their current or past clients to independently verify whether they are the real deal.

If you're searching for an FL, simply complete a brief profile about yourself and what you're looking for. After confirming potential matches' availability, we will email you up to three vetted FL referrals within three business days.

GigX.com/Network

GigX contains a directory of, as of this publication, over 900 FLs, who pay for inclusion in the directory using a monthly membership model. You can search and filter the directory by several factors, including category, title, role, industry, country, location, company size, years in industry, country(countries) where worked, and language proficiency. The system allows you to reach out to them by phone, visiting their website, or messaging them through the site.

InterimExecs.com

InterimExecs assigns members of their vetted "RED Team" to interim executive engagements. This is for people who need to find an interim executive, whether full-time or fractionally. For more details, check out my interview with the founder and CEO, Robert Jordan.[35]

To use them, simply fill out the form on their website, and someone from their team will get on the phone with you to learn more about who you are, what you're looking to accomplish, and what you need. They will then introduce you to one or more interim executives whom they feel may be a good fit for you.

If you want to engage one of the members of their RED Team, you will do so through InterimExecs throughout the

---

35 "How to Find an Interim Executive When You Need One ASAP: Interview with Bob Jordan," *Win Win—An Entrepreneurial Community* podcast, episode 70, November 17, 2020, https://podcasts.apple.com/us/podcast/070-how-to-find-interim-executive-when-you-need-one/id1465488607?i=1000499025559.

engagement and their team will support you and the interim executive during the process.

Fractional Integrator Directory

Mark C. Winters, coauthor of *Rocket Fuel: The One Essential Combination That Will Get You More of What You Want from Your Business*, and founder of www.RocketFuelUniversity. com, has spent several years compiling a list of Fractional Integrators for businesses searching for them. You can obtain the most up-to-date copy of this list by visiting his website.[36]

Other Places to Look

- There are several startups from the private equity world that connect executives available for freelance work and that may include actual Fractional Leadership work in some instances. Check out places like www.Paro.io, www.bolster.com, www.fracti.onl and www.GoCatalant. com for examples.

- Search Google. ;-)

---

36 https://www.markcwinters.com/rocket-fuel/fractional-integrators-list-download/.

Five Questions You Must Ask Yourself before Talking with Your First FL Candidate

1. What industry experience do you need, if any?

2. What situational experience, if any, do you need? This may include things like M&A transactions, product rollouts, and much more.

3. What is your workstyle and what are your core values? In other words, what are the core values someone must have to be a good fit with you and your team?

4. What time commitment do you need?

5. What is your monthly, annual, or engagement-long budget for this engagement?

Five Questions for Your FL to Determine if It's a Good Fit

1. Do they have the industry experience you need (manufacturing, retail, e-commerce, service, etc.), if any?

2. Do they have the situational experience (e.g., M&A transactions, product rollouts, etc.) you need?

3. Does their workstyle represent a core-values fit with you?

4. Can they offer you the time commitment you need?

5. Is their rate within your budget?

Six Questions for Potential FL's References, i.e., Current or Past FL Clients

1. What did you engage the FL to do and what was your relationship with him or her in that engagement?

2. How would you describe your overall satisfaction with the engagement?

3. Please share a story or two when the FL provided excellent service.

4. Please share a story or two when the FL disappointed you. How did they respond?

5. Would you select this FL again knowing what you know today? Why or why not?

6. Please share something else to backfill my understanding, something I should know but didn't ask about.

Points to Consider Addressing in Your Written Agreement with Your FL

1. Both parties' legal names

2. Start date of the engagement

3. The specific accountabilities or deliverables, and by when they're due

4. Time commitment

5. Reporting obligations

6. Compensation

7. Frequency of payment

8. Method of payment

9. What happens if payments are not made on time

10. How are expenses handled

11. How vacation is handled, both theirs and yours

12. Term and termination methods

13. Notice method/requirements

14. Applicable law, how any disputes are to be resolved

Simple Fractional Leader Agreement

This agreement is based on the one I use with my own clients. Some use no written agreement at all, and others use much more extensive ones. I also have a simple, separate nondisclosure agreement I use with clients to whom this is important. Please reach out to me through www.FractionalLeadership. io and I am happy to share a copy of that.

There are many other provisions people commonly put in their agreements, including choice of law, notice requirements, and noncompete or nonsolicit clauses. But personally, I find that the main purpose of the agreements is to get on the same page about the most important practical elements on how the engagement will work. So I have simplified my own agreement to keep it no-frills and under one page. This book certainly does not contain any legal advice, but if you find this agreement, or some part of it, useful, more power to you.

FRACTIONAL LEADER AGREEMENT

This Fractional Leader Agreement ("Agreement") is entered into as of [___], 20XX (the "Effective Date") between ABC Company LLC ("Client"), a [Name of State] limited liability company with offices at [___], and [FL's Company Name], a [Name of State] limited liability company with offices at [___] ("FL," and, collectively with Client, the "Parties").

In consideration of the following mutual covenants ,and other good and valuable consideration ,the receipt and sufficiency of which are hereby acknowledged ,the parties hereto agree as follows:

1. Services. FL shall provide Fractional Leadership services ("Services") to Client consisting of: (a) [Deliverable #1]; (b) [Deliverable #2]; (c) [Deliverable #3]; (d) [Deliverable #4]; and (e) [Deliverable #5]. It is understood that the Services will require an average of one business day per week.

2. Compensation and Expenses. Client shall compensate FL $[___] per month in the form of two $[___] payments per month, due to FL in advance, no later than the first and fifteenth of each calendar month. With respect to FL vacations, the Parties agree to schedule an additional day of service to make up for the vacation day. Client shall reimburse FL for travel expenses, including reimbursement for miles driven at the then-current Internal Revenue Service standard mileage rates, upon submission of a separate invoice for such expenses, payable on a net 15 basis.

3. Hold Harmless and Indemnification. Client shall fully defend, indemnify, and hold harmless FL from claims of any kind whatsoever, whether brought by an individual or other entity, or imposed by a court of law or by administrative action of federal state, or local governmental body or agency, arising out of, in any way whatsoever, any acts, omissions, negligence, or willful misconduct on the part of Client, its officers, owners, personnel, employees, agents, contracts, invitees, or volunteers. This indemnification applies to and includes, without limitation, penalties, fines, judgments, awards, decrees, attorneys' fees, and related costs/expenses, and any reimbursements to FL for all legal fees and expenses it incurs.

4. Term and Termination. This Agreement shall be valid from the Effective Date until either (1) both Parties consent in writing to the termination thereof or (2) either Party terminates the Agreement with written notice to the other (for which email notice shall suffice) at least one month in advance of the effective date of such termination.

IN WITNESS WHEREOF, a duly authorized representative of each of the undersigned has executed this Agreement as of the day and year first above written.

ABC COMPANY LLC   [FL'S COMPANY NAME]

By: _____   By: _____

Name: Name:

Title: Title:

Acknowledgments

THIS BOOK COULD NEVER HAVE COME TO FRUITION without the help of people too numerous to name. I name some here at the risk of unintentionally omitting certain individuals. For that I apologize in advance. It is not a reflection of any lack of gratitude or diminution in the magnitude of their contributions.

First, I must thank my wife, Melissa, for her love, patience, support, and understanding as I ran one business, built another business, and simultaneously worked on this book. She is the greatest human being I know, and I am forever grateful to God for allowing me to meet her and share my life with her and our children.

Thank you to the many business owners, leaders, and Fractional Leaders who shared their stories and insights with me to help business owners understand the world of Fractional Leadership. These individuals include (in alphabetical order by first name) Andrea Perales, Bill Stratton, Brad Martyn, Burke Autrey, Chris Coluccio, Christal Jackson, Cory Warfield, Cyndi Gave, David Bourke, Gary Braun, Gino Wickman, Jamie Munoz, Jason Prentice, Jennifer Zick, Jerry Rick, Jill Young, Jim Muehlhausen, Kevin McMahon, Kwame Christian, Esq., Marisa Smith, Mark O'Donnell, Natalie Franke, Rachel Beider, Rick Wilson, and Teresa Renaud. This book would have been a lot less enlightening and a lot more boring without the anecdotes, insights, and case studies you shared with me.

I am grateful to all of my clients, members of the EOS community, and the Fractional Leaders and business owners I've met both online through Zoom calls and at networking meetings over the past several years for cumulatively adding to my understanding of entrepreneurial business, as well as how and where Fractional Leaders are a powerful tool in business owners' arsenal.

Thank you to all of those on my LinkedIn network who offered insights and opinions on what makes a Fractional Leader engagement work or not work and title ideas. The crowdsourcing truly helped. And particularly large thanks go to Timera Garcia for suggesting what essentially became the title of this book.

I look forward to continuing to collaborate with an ever-widening circle of inspired entrepreneurs and trusted advisors in the years to come.

BEN WOLF is the founder and CEO of Fractional Leadership LLC (www.FractionalLeadership.io), which matches vetted, profiled executives with business owners for Fractional Leadership engagements. He is also the founder and CEO of Wolf's Edge Consulting, through which he and his team provide Fractional Integrator services to small and midsize businesses.

Previously, Ben built most of the operations at a healthcare startup from prelaunch till it became the largest organization of its type in New York State. He lives in Woodmere, New York, with his amazing wife and four awesome children. He previously practiced corporate restructuring and bankruptcy law at Kramer Levin Naftalis & Frankel in New York City.

CPSIA information can be obtained
at www.ICGtesting.com
Printed in the USA
BVHW040737161122
651046BV00006B/188/J